THE EUROPEAN CHALLENGE

THE EUROPEAN CHALLENGE

From Atlantic Alliance to Pan-European Entente for Peace and Jobs

by
Andre Gunder Frank

With a Foreword by
RICHARD J. BARNET

LAWRENCE HILL & COMPANY
Westport, Connecticut

First published in Great Britain in 1983 by Spokesman Press.

Published in the United States of America by
Lawrence Hill & Company, 520 Riverside Avenue,
Westport, Connecticut 06880.

1 2 3 4 5 6 7 8 9

Library of Congress Cataloging in Publication Data

Frank, Andre Gunder, 1929-
The European challenge.

Bibliography: p. 104.
1. Europe—Economic conditions—1945-
2. Europe—Politics and government—1945-
3. Europe—Foreign relations—United States.
4. United States—Foreign relations—Europe. I. Title.
HC240.F722 1984 338.94 84-6588
ISBN 0-88208-173-X (pbk.)

Printed in the United States of America

In memory of Dudley Seers who wanted to continue to contribute to the European challenge.

For my friends in Eastern Europe who unknowingly encouraged me in this direction and all those who strive for liberalisation there without concessions to reaction and to my friends in Western Europe who wrongly chastised me as a defeatist pessimist and to all those who strive for the maintenance of peace in Europe and its extension everywhere.

Acknowledgements

I am thankful to my colleagues and friends at the Institute for the Study of Labour and Economic Crisis in San Francisco, David Seddon in Norwich, Michael Ellman in Amsterdam, and Attila Agh in Budapest for helpful comments — and above all questions — on an earlier draft and to Peter Burgess in London for editorial changes; although I regret that I have been unable to make all the improvements they — and no doubt other readers — call for.

Contents

Foreword

Not so long ago the newspapers were filled with stories announcing the imminent death of NATO. The Atlantic Alliance, so the reporters and pundits had it, was after almost forty years about to come to an end. The dispute between Ronald Reagan, François Mitterand, Margaret Thatcher, and Helmut Schmidt about whether Europeans should arrange their affairs in such a way as to be dependent upon the Soviet Union for natural gas turned into a display of public acrimony. The leaders of the Western World seemed to be at each other's throats. The peace movement was putting millions on the streets in opposition to the NATO decision on so-called "theater" nuclear weapons.

Two years later the hysterical tone of the mainstream press in the United States has been replaced by complacency and relief. The Germans elected Helmut Kohl and the peace movement was unable to prevent the deployment of the first Pershing missiles. The British re-elected Margaret Thatcher and thereby gave a resounding rebuff to the unilateral nuclear disarmament of the Labour Party. Caspar Weinberger defeated E. P. Thompson in a debate at the Oxford Union by convincing the judges that the United States was morally superior to the Soviet Union. The world was back on track.

It is the great merit of Andre Gunder Frank's essay that it looks beyond the fashions of the moment to the underlying causes of the fundamental shift that is taking place in political and economic relations within the industrial world. For reasons that are spelled out in the book, the economic interests of the Europeans and Americans are diverging. This will be whatever the political complexion of governments that come to power in the United States or on the continent. The essay ought to help Americans understand feelings and concerns in Europe which are not well known here.

There are fundamental facts of history and geography which are part of the heritage of every European but not of Americans. Russia, whose vast expanse and mysterious ways, have always perplexed and on occasion alarmed people in western Europe is, nonetheless, a part of the continent, a fixture of the landscape. The same can not be said of the United States. At the end of the Second World War the foreign policy elite in the United States made a conscious decision that this nation should exercise hegemonic power over western Europe, for the alternatives were perceived to be Soviet hegemony or German hegemony. In those days most of the centrist politicians in western Europe agreed. United States support had helped to defeat formidable leftist and neutralist forces in each country in the western half of the continent. The Europeans would become protectorates of the United States. In return for a major defense commitment from the United States the world's most powerful nation would be given crucial decision-making power over the fate of Europe—in the military, political and economic spheres.

Forty years later the situation is quite different. As Frank shows, economic interests are diverging in quite specific ways among the industrial capitalist nations. What the United States could do when it was literally the only undamaged industrial nation in the world—the only nation to be enriched rather than bled white by war—is quite different from what it can do today. One of the fascinating questions raised by this study is why the United States continues to exercise political influence over the continent beyond anything which its comparative economic power would justify. The answer, it seems to me, lies in the divisions within Europe and the cultural and institutional lag which makes it difficult to act as if power had truly shifted.

But, as Frank reminds us, this is changing, too. His judgment that the two halves of Europe need each other economically and will be drawn together culturally and politically is one I share. It is a development that is in the interests of world peace and hence in the interests of the United States if this nation can develop an imaginative foreign policy to take account of the changing conditions. Unfortunately, our politicians seem frightened by these new developments, and they prefer to ignore them or lash out against them. The reintegration of Europe is a historic process that need not and must not be "anti-American."

Andre Gunder Frank's account of changing attitudes in Europe ought to be read in the light of significant changes here. The consensus behind NATO, once the sacred cow of the bipartisan foreign policy, is fast eroding in large measure because of the economic issues raised in the book but most significantly because of divergences in outlook about managing the common relationship with the Soviet Union. Since 1975 there has been a growing loss of confidence in American leadership. The vacillation of the Carter Administration and the belligerance of the Reagan Administration has led to a greater degree of independence in Europe because American policy seemed to be increasing the risks of war.

The famous missile deployment is likely to turn into a Pyrrhic victory. The pro-U.S. national security consensus is broken. The opposition in Britain and Germany are now committed to a quite different approach to security questions from that which the United States espouses. These differences in perspectives transcend traditional left-right politics. Franz Joseph Strauss is as likely—probably more likely—to make independent approaches to the Soviets for a modus vivendi in Europe as left-wing Social Democrats.

The reaction of conservatives in the United States to signs of European independence, which go far beyond the self-described peace movement, is to call for a unilateral withdrawal from Europe. If the continent is no longer a willing platform for fighting the cold war or a "limited" hot one, then our commitments to it, they say, do not constitute a foreign policy asset. If the Europeans won't pull their own weight, given the fact that they are richer, more technically advanced, and more populous than the Soviet Union, why should the United States continue to "defend" them? Let us pull our forces back and use them elsewhere in the world where we are not subject to European timidity.

This point of view, which is growing, is nothing other than traditional American isolationism. Despite a small pacifist wing of the isolationist movement that believed that nonmilitary international arrangements and institutions would serve the U.S. national interest, most isolationists were simply anti-Europe. The United States could be a hegemonic power everywhere else, but Europe was always trouble. It was the one place where it was hard for the United States to act unilaterally.

It will be a world tragedy if the movements for independence and "de-linking" of the fate of Europe and America proceed in separate directions. Just as the common obsession with solving nonproblems—stopping the Soviet invasion of western Europe in which no responsible military or political authority believes—is futile and divisive, so cooperation in dealing with the economic crisis that looms over the industrial world is vital—vital for itself and for the Third World. Relations between Europe and America have been poisoned by concentration on nonproblems and hopeless solutions. There is no "defense" in the nuclear age once a major war of any kind starts in Europe. A sensible deterrent policy is possible, but it must rest on economic and social strength and a more sensible military strategy—not on the threat to commit suicide and mass murder. Ideas for such a strategy exist. But the problems facing Europe and America are of a wholly different order from those the NATO bureaucrats spend their day on: How to defend the Elbe? Or the Rhine? With nuclear weapons? Without? The real threats have to do with the future of industrial civilization that still celebrates impotent nationalism in a world economy that is increasingly integrated and transnational. *The European Challenge: From Atlantic Alliance to Pan-European Entente* helps us begin to confront the real changes that have taken place in our world.

RICHARD J. BARNET

Preface to the American Edition

The European Challenge speaks to American concerns, even though it was written primarily for Europeans and with their peace movement in mind. It surveys the reasons for, and recent economic, strategic and other manifestations of, the deterioration of the Atlantic Alliance between America and Western Europe. It then proposes an increasing rapprochement and the reconstruction of historic ties between Eastern and Western Europe as an economically based realistic alternative and a major possible contribution to the prevention of nuclear war in and over Europe. But in so doing, this book also speaks to some important American concerns: the changing role, if not declining place, of the United States in theworld, and in particular, the deterioration of its Atlantic Alliance with Western Europe; the growing differences in American and West European perception of and relations with the Soviet Union and Eastern Europe, especially the threat of nuclear war and practical policies to prevent it, which Americans and Europeans also perceive differently; the often ill-perceived, or at least differently perceived, connections between military-strategic relations and political-economic ones; the continued development of the world economic crisis and the resultant pressures for protectionism and toward renewed political economic bloc formation; the growing demands everywhere, which the 1984 American election campaign expresses through the Democratic Party, for state intervention in trade and investment through "industrial policy;" and the limitations of this and other policies, especially when confined to national levels, in a world economy in crisis, which does not seem to be easily subject to national or even international policy control. With regard to practical politics and social movements, *The European Challenge* also raises questions for Americans regarding possible areas of cooperation, including the often underemphasized ones of economic policy, between the nuclear freeze, peace, and anti-interventionist movements in America and similar movements in Europe and the Third World. Richard Barnett, who has written a major study of American-European relations, has kindly agreed to write a forword to this American edition of my book. Therefore, I can safely leave to him the further elaboration of some of these American concerns and of this book's relevance to the American reader.

I may, however, take this opportunity to review for the American reader some developments of transatlantic and East-West European relations, and of their reflection in the press, since the European edition of this book was written in 1982. In the main, the tendencies outlined in this book have continued to develop in the same directions, despite some political attempts on both sides of the Atlantic and of Europe to retard or reverse them. Some political and journalistic highlights of the continuation of these tendencies were editorial headlines, such as "When Allies Diverge" (*International Herald Tribune,* 30 November 1983) and "The Atlantic Gets Wider" (*Financial Times,* 3 January 1984). An official in the U.S. State Department forecast "the shift of the center of gravity of U.S. foreign policy from the transatlantic relationship toward the Pacific basin, and particularly Japan . . . [as] the Pacific and clearly Japan are consistently taking on a more important role, at least in terms of the world economic situation. . . . The U.S. . . and our NATO allies, dealing more and more with their immediate difficulties, have tended to some degree imperceptibly to move further apart" (*International Herald Tribune*). Since 1980, some 85 percent of the growth of American imports has been from the Pacific area, rather than from Europe and Africa.

In the meantime, "the Atlantic gets wider" because, as the *Financial Times* (3 January 1984) editorializes, "On the more material questions of defense and economics, however, it is by no means clear that we are bound by a common interest. The American shield now looks, to a significant and vocal minority, more like an American threat. . . . The European governments should take a lead in seeking more constructive means of adjustment. . . . Russia's self-confessed economic weakness is, in fact, an important opportunity for the West, as the European business community has always recognized, but it will take courage to speak up for constructive contacts." So President Reagan's closest ideological and political ally in Europe, Prime Minister Margaret Thatcher, condemned his invasion of Grenada as illegal, immoral, and politically unacceptable and turned around to make a state visit to Hungary and then to pay her respects in Moscow on the occasion of the funeral of Andropov because, as she said, beyond all ideological and other differences with the Soviet Union and Eastern Europe a European dialogue with them is necessary. For her West German conservative colleague and ally, Chancellor Helmut Kohl, even more than talk appears necessary. Kohl gave a state guarantee to a one billion mark credit to East Germany, which was negotiated by none other than the archconservative Franz Joseph Strauss of Bavaria and which is to be administered by a Bavarian bank. The British Labour Party's opposition leader, Neil Kinnock, is calling for an Assembly of Europe with attendance also by nonmembers of the European Economic Community and closer economic links as well as more political dialogue between Western and Eastern Europe.

On the other hand, in Southern Europe the Socialist Party governments or heads of government in France, Italy, Spain, Portugal, and Greece have adopted "a pragmatic line [whose] realpolitik comes before ideology," as the *New York Times* (*International Herald Tribune,* 5 December 1983) has astutely observed. This "realism above everything else" has in no way changed the pro-American alignment or endangered U.S. military interests. On the contrary, the French Socialist President Mitterand has been more Atlanticist than his conservative predecessor and has led the European field in following President Reagan, with the other Socialists, Craxi, Gonzales, Soares, and Papandreou, not far behind.

Demonstrably and symptomatically, and unlike their conservative colleagues in Britain and Germany, none of these men appeared at Andropov's funeral in Moscow. Of course, none of these Socialists, unlike Thatcher and Kohl, is quite beyond reproach by the domestic opposition for possible pussyfooting with communism or the Soviet Union; and all of them still need maximum political leeway to impose economic austerity measures at home without quite admitting it. Maintaining their best Atlantic behavior in foreign affairs therefore shields them a bit on their still-exposed right flank. But once they, too, have done their necessary job of imposing austerity at home, and this becomes plain for all to see, even these Socialist heads of government—if they survive that long—may be able politically to afford to join the North European move to more Europeanist positions and policies.

These political and journalistic highlights barely reveal the continued economic, strategic, political, social, and ideological shifts of the continental plates underlying the Atlantic and Europe. "When Allies Diverge" was the title of an editorial commenting on an opinion poll: "what comes through clearly is a very big and important difference between how Americans view their security, and the prospect of war, and how the European allies and the Japanese see the situation.... The American vision of the world today is not really that of the allies. Policy divergence follows the perceptual gap. The situation is getting worse. The alliance is in trouble because its institutions of common action no longer rest upon a foundation of agreement on what the threat is, how grave it is and what should be done about it. . . . There lies the problem" (*International Herald Tribune,* 30 November 1983).

The international opinion poll taken by the Atlantic Institute-Louis Harris found that during the last year alone popular confidence in cooperation with the United States fell by 25 percent in Western Europe as a whole and by 35 percent in West Germany, where the desire for continued dialogue and contacts with the Soviet Union increased as a response, especially among conservatives, to displace relations with America as the first concern. In Italy and the Netherlands the trend was similar, albeit less pronounced; and in Japan, where there was no comparable poll for the previous year, "contacts with the Soviet Union (33 percent) were clearly preferred over all other options." Only in the United States was transatlantic security deemed more important than the year before, and there it clearly reflected the sharp rise in the fear of war, that is shared by West Europeans, but which expresses itself in increasingly divergent policy options on the two sides of the Atlantic. One third of Italians support unilateral nuclear disarmament, and the British Labour Party has turned against the Trident submarine and other nuclear defense options. The West German Social Democratic Party, which, under the leadership of then Chancellor Helmut Schmidt, first launched the idea of placing the new American Pershing II and cruise missiles in Europe, reversed themselves completely and at their October 1983 congress voted overwhelmingly against this stationing, leaving Schmidt in a minority of only six votes in favor of deployment.

Yet even Schmidt has warned that the "egoistic economic policies" of Washington are now a greater danger to the coherence and political stability of the Atlantic Alliance and could soon ruin it (*International Herald Tribune,* 16 January 1984). For their part, the Americans continue to press the Europeans to spend more money on conventional (read American) weapons for NATO and their own defense, while the Europeans increasingly argue that they can ill afford such increased military expenditures and certainly do not have the dollar foreign exchange to purchase them in the United States, which already sells five times as much arms as it buys in NATO. Thus, Henry Kissinger notes that Americans and Europeans are "lulled by complementary illusions," European leaders still want to make believe in the credibility of the by-now threadbare American nuclear deterrent, while American officials seek to sell more conventional weapons to Europeans who want to cut military spending (*International Herald Tribune,* 19 January 1984). A former Kissinger aide, William Hyland, goes further and says that "serious, thoughtful people in the United States" now doubt the value of staying in NATO; and "an important American general, known for his extravagant talk, took bets that the United States will quit the alliance by 1990—just six years away—in revulsion against the Europeans" (*International Herald Tribune,* 18 January 1984). It was the Europeans, both West and East, who were most insistent at the European Security Conference in Madrid (the continuation of the process started in Helsinki) that the proposals for the establishment of "confidence building measures" at the 1984 conference in Stockholm be taken seriously; it is the Europeans who most insist that Stockholm and Vienna be used to renew the superpower negotiations for arms control that were broken off at Geneva. The appointment of Britain's Lord Carrington (who was a former "wet" softie in Mrs. Thatcher's conservative cabinet) to succeed the Atlanticist hawk Joseph Luns as secretary-general of NATO has also been viewed as an indication and an instrument of strengthening a more independent European voice and resisting the tough American anti-Soviet line within the Alliance (*Time,* 16 January 1984).

The often underlying conflicts of economic interests between Europe and America, which are emphasized in this book, have also continued to grow and to generate renewed complaints and clashes. "You don't print money anymore, you import it," Helmut Schmidt told the Americans. They are running not only a $200 billion domestic budget deficit that drives up interest rates, thereby attracting European money, but also a nearly $100 billion foreign trade deficit, which the United States can afford only as long as the dollar is high and remains the world's principal reserve currency. In furious reaction, French Finance Minister Jacques Delors has already proposed that Europeans must consider some kind of curbs and penalties against the export of West European capital to the United States, which he estimates at some $150 billion during the past year. These foreign funds permit the Americans to engage in their extravagant defense and other expenditures with the money of other people, whose resentment of this is fed by their own thereby increased austerity. At the same time, the United States has further restricted the import of European specialty-steel (and Japanese, Brazilian, etc. steel); and the Europeans threaten to retaliate with import restrictions on American petrochemicals and other products of heavy industry. The Americans, with the powerful farm lobby getting up steam, continue to complain about the subsidy and protection of their agriculture in Europe, where there are also powerful farm interests; and the Americans threaten to retaliate by raising the tariff on European wines, which compete with the growing California wine industry. European trade with the Soviet Union and Eastern Europe, and especially European government credit guarantees and subsidies of this trade, which is vital for both parts of Europe, remain a major and growing bone of contention with the Americans, who continue to try to use the CoCom (Coordinating Committee on East-West trade in strategic goods) in Paris and the licensing of U.S. multinational technology to tie the Europeans' hands. The European response, even by a British Conservative Party minister, is to reject American "extraterritorial" legislation and rulings and to assert British and European sovereignty and independence in matters of intra-European trade.

Renewed recognition of the need for and desirability of increased trade and other peaceful relations within Europe and particularly between Eastern and Western Europe continues to grow in all parts of Europe. The above-mentioned one billion mark credit and negotiations for an additional credit are indications and instruments of this rapprochement. So are other bilateral contacts between West and East Germany, including a cordial meeting in Moscow between their respective heads of government, Kohl and Honecker. The latter has stressed several times that the deployment of new American missiles in West Germany need not poison good intra-German relations in other areas of common interest. Indeed, the *Washington Post* (*International Herald Tribune,* 22 February 1984) reports that "East Germany becomes the strongest advocate of detente and cooperation with the West, spurred by public discontent with the economy and anxiety about nuclear weapons. . . . For the East Germans more profitable relations hold out the promise of a relaxation of years of rigid austerity measures." The other side of this coin is that American spokesmen, and also some in France, have voiced the concern that the West German peace movement is little more than a smokescreen for German reunification, which some continue to regard as a threat in both West and East. Moreover, the retaliatory deployment of new Soviet missiles in East Germany has drawn the open opposition of Romania and supposedly the quiet chagrin of some political currents in Czechoslovakia and in the German Democratic Republic itself.

Also, the new Soviet premier's concern with domestic economic problems and intra-European detente, which Chernenko displayed publicly at the ceremonies and receptions of European leaders for the funeral of his predecessor Andropov, is evidence of some basis for increased and improved intra-European relations. So are the continued pressures for and steps toward economic and administrative reform in various countries of Eastern Europe. At the same time, the crisis-generated pressure for greater Comecon integration in Eastern Europe and the Soviet Union does not necessarily pose an alternative, but may offer a complement to East-West trade, since many intra-Comecon exports, especially from Eastern Europe to the Soviet Union, are based on technological and other inputs from Western Europe. Therefore, the recent decline of East European imports from the West, also crisis generated, and the use of the resulting trade surpluses to start paying off the accumulated debt to the West, can provide the basis for more stable future East-West European economic and other relations over the long run. Analogously, the continuing and indeed growing obstacles to West European economic integration within the EEC and its expansion to include Spain, Portugal, and Turkey need not be an indication that an even larger Europe that would include the East is necessarily illusory. On the contrary, more East-West European economic ties and political dialogue, even through a criss-cross network of bilateral relations throughout all of Europe, can be a means of overcoming or at least bypassing some of the obstacles to integration within a smaller Western Fortress Europe—and such a reemergence of pan-European relations can be a major step toward defusing the growing threat of nuclear war.

A. G. F.
Amsterdam
February 22, 1984

THE EUROPEAN CHALLENGE

"The days of the old 'Atlantic' system are over" — Four Western Foreign Policy Institutes.

"The Alliance as it was is no longer" — *International Herald Tribune.*

"A major crack in the Soviet block has become the occasion for nearly as big a crack in the West" — *The Guardian.*

"Security in the West, Business in the East" — *Neue Zürcher Zeitung.*

Introduction:

The Transformation in the Balance of Power between Europe and America

President Reagan's June 1982 decision to prohibit European subsidiaries and licencees of American firms to deliver components for the Soviet-European gas pipeline brought long simmering conflicts within the Atlantic Alliance to a head and into the headlines. America's European allies were especially angered by the fact that the pipeline decision was taken only days after American implicit promises not to do so at the June 1982 Western economic summit at Versailles and NATO summit at Bonn, and it provoked the resignation of Secretary of State Alexander Haig in protest. The Europeans sent several ministerial delegations to the United States to protest against the violation of their sovereignty and on his American tour West German Chancellor Helmut Schmidt demanded the retraction of the decision and the limitation of the damage already done to Atlantic Alliance relations.

The *Financial Times* (30 June, 1982) editorialised under the title "Europe at odds with Reagan":

> "It is a measure of the perturbed state of the Western world that the leaders of the European Community at an EEC summit . . . should have drafted communiques concerned predominantly with external affairs. The theme which united both main statements — on the crisis in Lebanon and on US-Common Market relations — is the rift which has suddenly re-opened between the American and the European halves of the NATO alliance. The virtuous-sounding undertakings of the Versailles summit are now shown up to have been little more than a papering-over of that rift.
>
> "Painful developments have taken place since they were made. The US has turned a blind eye to an Israeli invasion of Lebanon. Mr Alexander Haig, an unsatisfactory US Secretary of State, who,

> nevertheless, provided a link between Europe and the Reagan Administration, has resigned. The US has attacked European sales of steel to America with anti-dumping levies. The US has abruptly blocked European subsidiaries and licensees of US companies from participating in the Russian gas pipeline project. And in the background, the US monetary squeeze has re-asserted itself, driving dollar interest rates and the dollar exchange rate upwards. In Europe there is not only anger about these developments in themselves but also a mounting disquiet about the US administration which has unleashed them."

The West German Minister of Economics, Otto Graf Lambsdorff, warned in the *Washington Post* that "the West European reaction to the embargo decision, however, should give the White House cause to reconsider ... The West Europeans are in agreement ... The principle of extra-territoriality in US government decisions is unacceptable to us. It violates our sovereignty. Therefore, we have to reject it ... Above all, the harsh words of President Reagan's closest ally, British Prime Minister Margaret Thatcher, are an alarming signal of discontent within the alliance" (reprinted in *International Herald Tribune*, 1 August, 1982).

This book examines this growing disarray and discontent within the Atlantic Alliance and the transformation of the balance of power between Europe and America, especially in the economic field. This is followed by a review of the growing political economic conflicts in the Soviet Union and Eastern Europe and by an examination of the economic basis that they offer for Pan European political economic and strategic alternatives and possibilities for the world peace movement and a European de-nuclearised zone, which could help avert nuclear war in Europe.

In early 1981 the growing rift in the Atlantic Alliance was the subject of an important study issued jointly by the four most influential American, British, German and French foreign policy institutes, entitled *Western Security: What has changed? What should be done* (Kaiser 1981):

> "The days of the old 'Atlantic' system, based on US predominance

and its corollary, European reluctance to take wider responsibilities are over" (p.17).

"It is particularly striking to note that the prevailing debate over the future of American-European relations (as well as East-West relations) revolves around two opposite nostalgias: on the European side, it is the nostalgia for the far-reaching detente hoped for in the early 1970s . . . A similar phenomenon is at work in the United States. Here, a growing aspiration is to return to the era of US supremacy and absolute leadership in world affairs. This is translated in the resurgent tendency to consider every event in the world in purely East-West terms, and the use of force as the panacea for most such issues" (p.18).

"The common denominator is the relative decline of US power over the past decade and a half (in political and economic terms in the first instance, in military terms in the second) . . . The transformation of the balance of power between Europe and America has been most spectacular in the economic field. Here the American supremacy of the immediate post-war period has been replaced by a situation in which the European Community as a whole has become as rich as the US and often more competitive on the world market. As a result, the ability of the United States to influence European policy in accordance with its own interests has sharply declined. Conversely, the Europeans have shown a greater willingness and ability to defend their own interests against those of the United States, where these have diverged. Examples are the German-American quarrel over the 'locomotive theory' and the European-American controversy over nuclear energy and non-proliferation. In the monetary field, the creation of the European Monetary System was aimed to a large extent at shielding Europe from the consequences of the decline of the dollar-based international monetary system" (p.12).

"Militarily, Europe as a whole remains dependent on the nuclear guarantee provided by the United States . . . [Nonetheless] despite the decision laboriously reached by NATO in December 1979, the modernisation of long range theatre nuclear forces (LRTNF) in Europe remains in doubt . . . Similarly, disagreements over the Middle East and policy towards Iran also sharpened" (p.8).

"Divergences bear not just on isolated problems, but on a whole spectrum of issues, ranging from defence to economics and basic foreign policy . . . Because of the magnitude of these disagreements and divisions, actual and potential . . . the authors have decided jointly to write this Report" (p.9).

This increasing tension in and threat to the Atlantic Alliance is widely echoed elsewhere. For instance the

American magazine *Newsweek* and the *International Herald Tribune* (25 January, 1982) editorialised under the title "The Alliance as it was is no longer" and suggest that "perhaps it was always doomed . . . We could have been living in a nuclear-armed fool's paradise all these years. But that was then. The question now is what variation on the alliance or substitution for it can fill the void". The *Financial Times* (14 April, 1982) informs that "Professor Hedley Bull, a prominent international affairs specialist, argued that the countries of Western Europe are now perfectly capable of providing for their own defence, and that they must do so because of the underlying divergence of interests between them and the United States. In particular . . . over the Soviet Union". *The Guardian* (23 December, 1981) commented on military rule in Poland and observed that "the trouble with East-West crises, is that they all too rapidly turn into West-West crises. So it is again". Another aspect of the situation is that "trade problems between Japan and the West are much worse than most people realise and could . . . lead to a breakdown of free trade between Japan and the US and Japan and Europe" (*Financial Times*, 26 January, 1982). The *International Herald Tribune* quotes an OECD official's evaluation of "the wave of protectionism spreading among Western industrial nations": "we are facing a situation potentially as dangerous as the 1930s" and the *Financial Times* (23 December, 1981) editorialises under the title "Sick patient, no cure": "the most depressing aspect of the latest [OECD] report is the virtual absence of all economic prescription . . . The need for economic co-ordination and guidance is much greater today than it was then, yet the OECD is apparently much less able to provide them". On the contrary, as the *International Herald Tribune* (11 May, 1982) headlines "Divided on Tactics in Recession, OECD Nations Take Separate Paths". The *Guardian* (19 February, 1982) quotes the then West German Chancellor Helmut Schmidt: "For my taste, there is too much talk about so-called strategic questions in the military and political field, and too little talk and too little co-operation in the economic field. We have not seen a world economic recession of this degree since the 1930s. One could easily turn this into a general depression of the Western world". (Subsequently, President Reagan's ban on foreign gas pipeline component deliveries to the Soviet Union led to a storm of European protest and the US Secretary of State's resignation.)

The above quotations and expressions of serious concern reflect world developments that cannot be brushed off lightly as accidental or momentary aberrations in an otherwise harmonious development. The background and causes of these recent and prospective developments should be sought in the long run development of the world economy, with its apparently regular long waves of economic growth alternating with relative stagnation or crisis, the tendency of hegemonic powers to decline first relatively and then absolutely — economically, politically, militarily and financially more or less in that order — in the course of successive crises, and their replacement by others who are more successful in adjusting to the exigencies and opportunities presented by renewed world economic crisis. Although this long run structure and development of the world economic and political system is beyond the immediate scope of this paper it is useful to keep it in mind as a backdrop of the recent development.

A related fundamental background if not cause of these shifts in world political economic power and international relations that are the centre of attention in this essay is the current world economic crisis, which must remain beyond our scope here (but which the present author has examined in recent books and articles, especially Frank 1980, 1981a, 1981b).* Briefly, it appears that since about 1967 the world capitalist economy — but with very far-reaching repercussions also in the socialist ones — has entered another of its periodically recurrent major crises of overaccumulation of capital. Profits, investment and economic and productivity growth rates decline or even turn negative and the most far-reaching economic, political

*References cited but not detailed in text are listed on p.89.

and social transformations must occur to lay the basis for a possible renewed period of expansion, such as that of the two post World War II decades. The last such crisis period lasted from 1914 to 1945 and included two world wars, two major socialist revolutions, the intervening Great Depression of the 1930s (but whose roots began earlier), the rise of fascism, and the final replacement of British by American hegemony. The analogous crisis of a century ago started in 1873 and was accompanied by the rise of monopoly capitalism, classical imperialism and renewed colonialism. In each of these — and also earlier — major crises capitalist competition became more acute as the growth of the world economic pie slowed down and political relations sharpened, leading for instance to

Table 1
Growth Rates of Real Output, 1960-1981
(per cent)

	Total		*Per Capita*		*Per Unit of Labour Input*	
	1960-1973 (1)	1973-1981 (2)	1960-1973 (3)	1973-1981 (4)	1960-1973 (5)	1973-1981 (6)
United States	4.2	2.3	3.0	1.2	3.1	0.9
Japan	10.5	3.8	9.3	2.9	9.9	3.6
Germany	4.8	1.9	3.9	2.0	5.8	3.3
France	5.7	2.5	4.6	2.2	5.9	3.4
United Kingdom	3.2	0.5	2.7	0.5	3.8	1.8
Italy	5.2	2.4	4.4	2.0	7.8	1.4
Canada	5.4	2.4	3.7	1.7	4.2	0.4

Note: Data for France, Italy, and the United Kingdom are based on gross domestic product. Data for the other countries are based on gross national product.

Source: Cols. 1, 2, 3, 4: International Monetary Fund, *International Financial Statistics*, various issues. 1981 partly estimated by the American Enterprise Institute. Col. 5 and col. 6, 1973-1979: John W. Kendrick, "International Comparisons of Recent Productivity Trends" in *Essays in Contemporary Economic Problems*, ed. William Fellner, 1981-1982 edition (Washington, DC: American Enterprise Institute, 1981), p.128. Col. 6, 1979-1981: Organisation for Economic Co-operation and Development, *Economic Outlook*, December 1981, p.46.

Source: *The AEI Economist* 1 May 1982.

renewed colonialism and major war in the last two crises respectively. Analogous convulsions during the present crisis should not be unexpected.

It is not necessary to share this author's interpretation of the nature of the world economic crisis to observe its all too visible manifestations, such as low growth rates, high unemployment, and changing competition and division of labour as well as distribution of political power. For instance, one of the most unpleasant manifestations of the current crisis, unemployment as officially registered but actually underestimated in the Western industrialised countries, more than doubled from less than 7 million in the 1967 recession to 15 million in the 1973-75 recession and then more than doubled again to 32 million at the time of writing in the 1979-82 recession, and it is certain to continue rising even further and by some predictions even to double once again.

The growth rates of production (or real output) and of productivity (or output per unit of labour input) in each of the major Western economies from 1960 to 1981 are summarised in the accompanying table, which also distinguishes between the periods before and after 1973, which marked the beginning of the first major post-war recession. The table shows that growth rates of output in the period since 1973 have fallen to half or less (excepting for the nearly half in the United States) of their averages for 14 years before 1973. Growth rates of labour productivity have fallen even more drastically in some economies to a third or a fourth (in Canada even a tenth) and in Germany and France to about 60 per cent of their previous averages. Productivity in the United States even declined absolutely during the three years 1978, 1979, and 1980, which overlapped with the renewed recession that began in 1979 (*Economic Report of the President*, February 1982, p.279).

The balance of power and the competitive rivalries within the West, however, are even more affected by the *difference* in growth rates of output and especially of productivity among the major Western economies. Over the entire period, the strongest and oldest economies, the United States and Britain, have had the lowest growth rates of both output and productivity. Until 1973, productivity in the major Continental European economies grew at nearly 6 per cent or almost twice as fast as the about 3 per cent annual growth in the United States (and 3.8 per cent in Britain); and in Japan productivity rose at 10 per cent per year, or nearly twice as fast again as in Continental Europe, or over three times as fast as the United States. When all the growth rates of output and productivity declined after 1973, Japan experienced the greatest absolute decline to 3.6 per cent and the United States the greatest relative decline to less than 1 per cent per year in productivity growth rates; while European rates only declined by less than half to over 3 per cent (and 1.8 per cent in Britain). Thus, as all of the economies slowed down, the Japanese, who still lag absolutely behind in the productivity race, were catching up more slowly with the Europeans, although both of them were still running faster than the United States. (For a discussion of relative productivity changes, see Kendrick 1981 and UNECE 1982 pp.73-97.) On the other hand, a recent European Economic Commission study suggests that this European productivity is concentrated in medium-technology industrial products, while European productivity and exports in the most advanced high-technology fields is seriously lagging — or comparatively declining — compared with both Japan and the United States over the past decade (*Business International*, 30 April, 1982; *Financial Times*, 6 December 1982).

These absolute and relative changes in growth rates of output and productivity have been the basis of substantial modifications of relative competitiveness in the world economy and in the balance of power and the degree of competition on the world market (as the foreign policy institutes observed); the devaluation of the dollar especially relative to the German mark and Japanese yen; the consequent relative changes in the 1970s of labour costs and earnings, which have risen particularly in

Europe and declined relatively and in some cases absolutely to lower levels in the United States; the shift in the direction of foreign investment across the Atlantic and of the shares in the Third World, and the transformation of the international balance of power and interests generally. A vivid manifestation of these transformations in the world economy is that at the end of the 1970s West Germany had overtaken the United States as the world's largest exporter, with Japan coming up fast behind.

The recent and prospective developments in the Atlantic Alliance and East-West and trilateral relations with Japan as well as North-South relations derive most immediately from recent changes in growth rates of economic, and especially industrial, production and productivity both over time and relatively as between different (country or regional) parts of the world economy. It is these economic changes which form the basis of "the transformation of the balance of power between Europe and America" as the four foreign policy institutes rightly observe. Since this shift has been from America to Europe and particularly to Germany, it is not surprising that the taste of the West German Chancellor is that economic matters should receive more attention and strategic ones, where America retains greater dominance, should be de-emphasised in international affairs.

Economic crisis and increasingly conflictual political relations are, however, also very manifest in and between the Soviet Union and Eastern Europe, China and Vietnam and within the Third World and particularly Western relations with all these regions. All of these are generating or aggravating conflicts of interest and new disputes about different alternatives for their resolution. We will examine some of these conflicts and alternatives with regard particularly to emerging strains within the Atlantic Alliance and Western Europe, difficulties within the Soviet Bloc and Eastern Europe, and European political economic policy alternatives particularly in Western Europe in the face of the world economic and political crisis.

Chapter One

West-West Conflict

As the four foreign policy institutes observe, the increasing divergences within the Atlantic Alliance bear not just on isolated problems but on a whole spectrum of issues, through which they are interlinked. For the sake of convenience, we may classify these issues, conflicts of interest and disagreements over policy in the Atlantic Alliance into three major groups: (1) economic policy, primarily in the United States and secondarily in Europe and Japan; (2) trade relations and policy, with regard to each other and to third parties, especially Japan and the Third World with particular emphasis on the Middle East; and (3) East-West relations.

Western Conflicts over Economic Policy

Conflicts of interest and disagreements over economic policy grew in the 1960s as the United States engaged in and increasingly abused inflationary finance of the Vietnam war, which flooded the world with dollars that Europe was obliged to accept and hold because the dollar was "as good as gold" as the only international reserve currency, even though its value increasingly declined and the Americans used newly printed and devalued dollars to buy up European industry virtually free of charge through what was still called "American foreign investment". De Gaulle reacted by cashing French held dollars at the US Treasury for gold. As the American ability to back the dollar with gold declined at the same time as the competitiveness of its exports did (as observed above) and the 1969-70 recession aggravated matters further,

President Nixon took the dollar off gold on 15 August, 1971 and began effectively to devalue the dollar. This measure laid the basis for a major American drive to increase exports, especially of agricultural products and military hardware, in order to restore at once US companies' balance sheets and the US balance of trade and payments, which had seriously deteriorated. These measures were quite successful particularly in 1972 and to varying degrees later in the 1970s.

However, this American economic offensive was undertaken at the expense of the Japanese (who called its initiation "Nixon shokku" especially inasmuch as they were initially penalised by a discriminatory 10 per cent export surtax) and the Europeans. Despite some adjustments, their exchange rates remained effectively pegged to the dollar by the Bretton Woods (1944) and Smithsonian (1972) agreements, which exposed their economies to the vicissitudes of the American economy and dollar, and especially to speculation with their currencies, which their central banks were obliged to try — unsuccessfully — to counteract by buying and selling these currencies on the open market. Therefore, on 19 March, 1973 the post-war system of fixed exchange rates was abandoned and replaced by one of flexible exchange rates in which all the currencies floated up and down against each other in response to supply and demand. It was hoped that this floating flexibility would take the wind out of speculators' sails, but it only made speculation steadier and reduced sudden runs on the banks. Changes in the now flexible exchange rates helped to act as shock absorbers in the international transmission of waves of inflation and deflation, which mostly originate in the United States. However, this partial protection of the national economies has been bought at the cost of fluctuations that render all price and cost calculations insecure. Accordingly, West Germany sought to dilute the effects of these shocks and uncertainties on itself by spreading them wider over her European trading partners' economies. The solution, which Germany bought at the cost of other economic guarantees to her major trading partners, was first the "snake" (1972) and then the EMS or European Monetary System (in 1979) in which the French, Benelux, later the Italian and some other currencies fluctuate within a maximum and minimum band of rates and wiggle in unison against the dollar like a snake. The EMS is designed essentially to protect Germany and France from fluctuations in the dollar, the vagaries of the American economy, and US economic policy. Britain has steadfastly refused to join in Germany's snake and EMS embrace.

The devaluation of the dollar, to which many other currencies elsewhere in the world remained pegged in fact if not in law, did much to restore US competitiveness in Europe and third markets and to raise the cost of European and Japanese exports in the US. On the other hand, it cheapened the purchase price of US assets for the Europeans and the Japanese. These complementary factors plus the elevation of wage rates in Europe/decline of wage costs in America relative to each other tended to reverse the flow of foreign investment across the Atlantic and to a lesser degree across the Pacific, so that foreign investment in the United States rose significantly during the 1970s, while some American investment was repatriated from abroad. The manufacture of German Volkswagens and Japanese TV sets in the US are well known examples of the former and the divestiture of Chrysler subsidiaries in Europe of the latter.

The common recession in 1973-75 and the weak recovery, especially in much of Europe, from 1975-79, the continuing inflation throughout, and the renewed recession and American policy since then have served to generate or strengthen other major conflicts of interest and policy disagreements. Some of these have been more out in the open than others. Among the latter is perhaps that of the price of oil. It has been suggested that the American response to European economic challenge was deliberately to penalise and weaken the Europeans and Japanese again by obliging them to pay more for the oil on whose import they (and the Japanese for nearly 100 per cent) are much more dependent than the US. American oil production maintained the domestic price at about half the level to which it was elevated in 1973-74 and again 1979 by OPEC and other oil producers — and mostly American owned Seven Sister major oil companies, whose profits rose spectacularly — and, it is sometimes claimed, by American government connivance or agreement. What is a matter of public record is that the then US Secretary of State, Henry Kissinger, was the first to propose a floor price for oil, under which it should not be allowed to sink again. It is also a matter of public knowledge that during the mid 1970s European and Japanese resistance to American pressures weakened again in public international conferences and apparently in negotiations behind closed doors.

Nonetheless, and counter to the expectations of many — and hopes of some? — American dependence on oil imports and their balance of payments costs was not quickly reduced but rather the opposite; and Germany and Japan weathered the oil price storm by increasing their exports despite strong currencies, particularly to the OPEC Middle East and the Socialist countries. As a result, they achieved a large balance of trade and some balance of payments surpluses in the mid 1970s. The Americans were pursuing relatively deflationary monetary and fiscal policies, supposedly to combat inflation during and after the 1973-75 recession. Since these policies put a brake on the recovery of the world economy, the Americans began to argue that the countries with a balance of payments surplus and a lower rate of inflation should prime the economic pump through reflation — which the Americans themselves refused to do — and become the "locomotive" to pull the world economy out of the doldrums. This American locomotive theory and its subsequent elongation into a convoy theory became major issues at the 1977 and 1978 economic summit meetings. The Germans and Japanese resisted the American pressure and rebutted their argument with the contention that their economies were too small to serve as locomotives for the world and that any effort to do so would only lead to domestic inflation. That is, reflation in these smaller national economies would price them out of the competitive world market and destroy their balance of payments. The size and relative isolation from foreign trade of the American economy (although even there exports doubled from 5 to 10 per cent of GNP while they rose from 7 to 15 per cent in Japan over the decade of the 70s) and the still relatively dominant dollar reserve currency, allows the US to pursue its own economic policies to a considerable extent without too much regard for any repercussions at home of its effects abroad — and the devil take the hindmost elsewhere. But the smaller more trade dependent European and Japanese economies, whose currencies are only beginning to rival the dollar, still lack this degree of economic independence. (This fact of life is illustrated by the opposite but common negative international boomerang repercussions on their own economies of Thatcher's domestic deflation with a high North Sea petropound in Britain and Mitterrand's reflation with a twice devalued franc in France in the early 1980s and will form part of the basis of our discussion of European economic policy below.)

The continued relative economic independence of the United States and its damned if they do/damned if they don't repercussions on Europe and Japan (not to mention the still weaker Third World economies) also made itself felt through the increasingly serious conflicts of interest and policy disagreements first over American balance of payments deficits and then over skyhigh American interest rates. In the late 1970s, the growing American balance of payments deficits drove down the dollar to the increasing annoyance of the Europeans, whose competitiveness was thereby weakened. On both sides of the Atlantic, much of the reason for the American trade and payments deficit was attributed to growing and increasingly costly oil imports. The Europeans and Japanese began to demand effective restrictions of American consumption and importation of oil, while

President Carter claimed that he was quite unable to force his national energy (saving and alternative synfuels) programme on an unwilling Congress and public, not to mention on the unco-operative oil companies and their powerful allies. In fact Carter's programme was a total failure as American oil dependence increased rather than decreased; and the Europeans vainly cried in the wind.

The turnaround on the US balance of payments and the effects of US economic policy on Europe and Japan came not as a change of policy but from a downturn of the underlying economic cycle. In mid 1979 the long awaited recession arrived in America. After a partial and brief recovery during late 1980 and early 1981, the recession became much deeper again in the United States and spread to Europe, Japan, and the rest of the world in 1981 and 1982. One result was that the consumption, import, price, and purchase cost of oil plummeted as a world-wide oil glut replaced its supposed scarcity. The American balance of payments deficits declined through lower import demand and expenditures on oil and other commodities (with raw materials in mid 1982 at so far rockbottom prices). The new American administration instituted its so-called new Reaganomic monetarist and supply-side policies, which (like Thatcherism in the UK) simply carried to their logical conclusion the policies begun during the preceding administration. However, Reagonomics — also like Thatcherism before it — has not succeeded (Frank 1982), in particular in reducing government budget deficits, which have instead grown to over $100 billion in the US and obliged the government to borrow money on the open market to fill up this hole in its pocket, thereby helping to drive up the interest rate cost of the money borrowed by itself — and everybody else. The American shift from negative interest rates (that were lower than the rate of inflation for most of the 1970s) to real interest rates of 6, 7 and up to 10 per cent has attracted a flood of money into the dollar, whose value rose again on most foreign exchange markets; and it has obliged everybody else either to let their own currencies fall through the floor thereby feeding inflation or to follow the American suit in raising interest rates and the cost of borrowing, thereby choking off investment in an already very recessive national and world economy.

The Europeans and Japanese are objecting, again, this time because the American dollar and the rate of interest are too high. This issue has replaced the previous ones as the major bone of contention between the Europeans and Japanese (who witnessed an unexpected massive capital flight from the therefore weak yen to higher interest currencies) and the Americans at the 1981 Ottawa and 1982 Versailles summits and numerous confrontations in between. However, this new conflict has become meshed with a whole spectrum of others with regard to issues of international trade policy between West and West, West and South, and finally West and East, which we may examine under these titles. One of the real but rarely mentioned links is that if interest rates are elevated by the budget conflict, that deficit in turn is elevated by increased defence spending in the American cold and economic war against the Soviet Union.

Western Conflicts over International Trade

West-West political economic conflicts of interest and policy disagreements or even battles are seriously shaking the Atlantic Alliance and Pacific relations. Indeed, the press headlines "US faces up to 'real threat' of trade war with Europe" (*Financial Times* 14 June, 1982) and "US-European Trade 'Shooting War' Feared" (*International Herald Tribune* 26 January, 1982) and speaks of an impending "breakdown of free trade" with Japan (*Financial Times*, 26 January, 1982).

The large Japanese trade surplus with the United States and Europe, and the repeated failures so far to eliminate or significantly reduce it, are well publicised in the West. What is not usually mentioned, however, is that Japan absolutely needs such a surplus in its American and European trade to cover its unavoidably huge deficits with its Middle Eastern and Asian suppliers of oil and raw materials, on which Japan is nearly 100 per cent import dependent; because these oil supply economies could not possibly absorb an equivalent sum of industrial imports from Japan in exchange. Therefore, the maintenance of this triangular trade relationship of deficit with the South and surplus with the West is literally a matter of life or death for Japan. No wonder then that Japanese officials and businessmen regard Western pressures to reduce the trade gap with them as the threat of a "trade war" in which they have no choice but to defend themselves at all costs.

The penetration of the American market by Japanese automobiles, TV sets, photographic equipment, and a myriad of other consumer products as well as steel and now even the threat from advancing Japanese high technology in electronic components and other producer goods is well known. So is the American insistence that Japan open its markets to imports of Western industrial goods and services, including banking. Less well known, except in Japan itself, are the huge Japanese imports of American agricultural products and the Japanese threats of consumer boycotts against American beef and oranges in retaliation against American pressures and complaints. However, when forced to choose among unpalatable alternatives, Japan is likely to prefer its economic and political alliance with the United States and the latter is increasingly leaning to a Pacific Rim strategy (to be examined below). In any event, the first option of United States policy with regard to its economic conflict with Japan has been to try to shift the burden of adjustment onto the back of Europe. If the Americans want to reduce their take of Japanese exports, let the Japanese sell them in Europe and elsewhere. The former French Ambassador to Japan observed that Japan needs the United States but believes it can do without Europe, a view confirmed by Japanese officials who privately regard Europe as a declining power whose national markets can be picked off one by one (*International Herald Tribune*, 27 May, 1982).

In the face of the increasing gravity of the economic

crisis in Western Europe, both absolutely and relatively to the US, (which recovered more in 1975-79 and again briefly in 1981), the Japanese export offensive in Europe is anything but welcome. On the contrary, the Vice-president of the European Economic Commission suggests that "trade problems between Japan and the West . . . could lead Europe to impose a total ban on Japanese imports", while in the Commission itself "Japan [is] seen as 'most vulnerable' to trade pressures . . . [and] liable to become the first victim of EEC trade curbs" (*Financial Times* 26 January and 8 February, 1982). Thus, the immediate economic basis for a major West-West political economic conflict between Europe and Japan already exists. A longer historical perspective should lead us to expect the most serious rivalry to develop between the principal contenders for the hegemony of the declining economic power in the world with a tactical alliance between the latter and one of the major contenders. Thus, previously Germany and America fought for the mantle of formerly Great Britain, which took the side of the ultimate winner in the conflict. Since similar situations had also developed earlier in world history, it would not be surprising if an analogous struggle and even the eventual victory of Japan in alliance with the declining America should develop in the future.

Other serious economic conflicts of interest and policy have developed between the United States and Western Europe over trade, particularly in petrochemical products, steel, and agricultural products and policy. The conflict about American oil consumption based on low domestic prices was not only about the American balance of payments and its effects on the dollar, but also about the European balance of payments and industrial profits in the face of American exports. Cheap oil in the US also subsidises American petrochemical products, which are either exported to Europe at prices with which European high oil cost producers cannot compete during a time of crisis in the world petrochemical industry, or the cheaper petrochemicals are converted into synthetic fibres for the textile and other industries that compete with European ones that are in an even deeper crisis. Understandably, European producers have raised alarmed cries of unfair competition from America and have used the Multifibre Agreement (MFA) to turn against more defenceless low labour cost textile exporters in Asia and Brazil to restrict their penetration of the European (and American) markets. Only the high dollar has reduced the American petrochemical/textile offensive.

Another major and growing conflict turns around steel. The world steel industry has been in the doldrums since 1973, and lagging or declining industrial investment and construction have sharply reduced steel demand and prices. Even after numerous steel mill shutdowns and/or labour dismissals, which have caused widespread social and political uproar all over Britain, Germany's Ruhr region, France's Lorraine, Belgium's Wallonia, Youngstown, Ohio in the US and elsewhere, much of the Western world's steel industry is working to only 60 to 80 per cent of capacity. In June 1982, capacity utilisation in the American steel industry dropped to 42 per cent, the lowest since 1938. Productivity in modern Japanese steel mills is over twice as high and labour costs less than half of the United States, with West European producers (except the British) in between. Accordingly, both Japanese and European steelmakers have been increasingly able to penetrate the American market to compensate a bit for the weakness of their own, (and the Europeans to cushion the effects of the necessary reorganisation of their steel industry through intra-EEC cartel like export quotas) but to the increasing chagrin and fury of American steel producers and workers. American steel consumption declined from about 120 million tons in 1973 to 100 million tons in 1975 and again in 1981. In the meantime, imports increased from 15 to 20 million tons, of which 6 million originated in Western Europe and raised its share of American consumption from 13 to 20 per cent (*Financial Times*, 10 June, 1982 citing the American Iron and Steel Institute and the US Department of Commerce). The

Americans charge that, beyond productivity advantages, the European exporters enjoy cost advantages from European government subsidies ranging from $50 to $300 for a ton of steel that sells in the US for $500. To counteract this foreign steel invasion, the US government proposed so-called trigger prices based on estimated Japanese and European costs of production below which it would restrict imports. This never very satisfactory measure went on and off and on again, until the present recession depressed the American domestic steel price itself below the trigger price, and the high dollar cheapened the American price of European steel, which then made the whole scheme increasingly inoperative. The American steel companies took matters in their own hands and pressed a whole series of cases before the American courts and the US Department of Commerce to enjoin European producers from dumping, as the Americans claim, steel on their market. With the June 1982 American rulings in favour of the American steel companies and the imposition of US countervailing duties against them, the steel war between Europe and America was on. Moreover, the new American steel duties deliberately hit at the weaker and more subsidised British, French and Belgian producers than at the stronger German ones and were designed to sow discord among the Europeans and to impede their effort at EEC common agreement on the necessary restructuring of the European steel industry and the multilateral sharing of the apparently obligatory reduction of their steel exports to the United States. Indeed, in the event West Germany did hold out against a common EEC agreement in Brussels until literally the eleventh hour of the American deadline for a settlement. The significance of these decisions and measures "goes well beyond the steel industry . . . and could well be applied to other products which benefit from government subsidies . . . (and) may set a precedent for other countries wishing to take action against subsidised imports". (*Financial Times*, 14 June, 1982.) The European Economic Commission (EEC) and its member governments sought countermeasures against the Americans. One of these was to take the dispute to GATT but at the very real risk of breaking the organisation or at least its effectiveness in safeguarding international trade as well in other goods if they cannot reach mutual agreement on steel. Another major field in which to look for them is agriculture — which by itself has been developing as an even more acrimonious Euro-American field of combat.

One of the paradoxes of world economic development is that the industrial capitalist economies are the most efficient producers of the major agricultural commodities, especially wheat and meat, but also other grains and dairy products. In addition, both the United States and Western Europe have been heavily subsidising their farmers for decades, who respond with huge food surpluses that either accumulate as mountains of wheat and butter or are exported at below market prices, or both. Although another world food shortage (not so much physically as because of high prices that the poor cannot afford) even deeper and longer than that of 1972-74 is looming for the later 1980s, the early 1980s have witnessed a massive increase of agricultural market surpluses, plummeting prices; and American farmers, who suffer from sky-high interest rates to boot, saw their incomes fall by more than one-third, signifying their worst crisis since the one of the 1930s, which was so dramatically depicted in John Steinbeck's *Grapes of Wrath.*

Throughout the 1970s and spurred on by the devaluations since 1971 and the conversion of "Food for Peace" (Public Law 480) to "Food is a Weapon" (US Secretary of Agriculture Earl Butz) and "Food is Power" (US Senator Hubert Humphrey), American commercial exports of agricultural products have soared. The Soviet "great grain robbery" and the increasing import dependence of much of the Third World on American wheat have received wide publicity, but less so the equally significant Japanese imports and West European dependence on American soybean and corn gluten feedstuffs to maintain their intensive feedlot livestock and the surplus producing European meat and dairy industries. Moreover, Brazil is challenging the American soybean supremacy. Therefore, the Europeans are set to reduce their dependence on American feedstuffs. To the fury of the Americans, the Europeans have also launched their own export drive in a weak international market, partly to bolster their own balance of payments and mostly to rid themselves of their own expensive agricultural surpluses and thereby to reduce the costs of the Common Agricultural Policy, contributions to which have become politically increasingly divisive and difficult to squeeze out among member states. Therefore, the Reagan administration has begun to "read the riot act" to the Europeans. It charges that the EEC share of world agricultural imports declined from 25 to 20 per cent of world imports while EEC exports rose from 9 to 11 per cent between 1973 and 1980 (*Financial Times*, 8 February, 1982). The Reagan administration is gunning for EEC agricultural exports to Third World markets in the Middle East and Latin America and charging that these exports, like those of steel, are unfairly and illegally subsidised by the EEC. The US Secretary of Agriculture told Congress that "we fear that the [EEC] is seeking to solve its internal agricultural overproduction and budget problems by converting CAP into a Common Export Policy based on extensive subsidies" (*International Herald Tribune*, 26 January, 1982).

In early 1982 warnings appeared that "Washington has gone on the offensive in this now major US-EEC dispute" (*Financial Times* 8 February 1982). Then, the press warned that agricultural products, which are the major US export today, may prove to be the most serious trade conflict yet with Western Europe after the latter had successfully resisted the American demands for reduced European agricultural subsidies and protection at the November 1982 GATT ministerial meetings and immediately afterwards. The US Secretary of Agriculture John Block threatened, "we have only one alternative. The alternative is to deviate temporarily from our free-market stance and engage in costly short-run trade wars. If that is what it takes to achieve the principles of free markets, then we will have to start looking more seriously in that direction" and massively dump $3 billion worth of the greater American stockpiles of agricultural products on the world market until the Europeans give up (*Financial Times* 23 November 1982). The imminent threat of this new trade war by the US Secretary of Agriculture was only defused until March 1983 by the conciliatory quiet diplomacy of US Secretary of State George Shultz and the intervention of the US Secretary of the Treasury with his European and Japanese Finance Minister colleagues. They want to try to work out a multilateral multi-issue settlement and possibly a new institutional world financial set up in the attempt to ward off a world financial crash and international trade breakdown in the wake of the inability of the world's three largest foreign debtor countries, Argentina, Mexico and Brazil, to pay their over US$200 billion of debts. Indeed, Reaganomic ideology and US intransigence, which were still manifest in American opposition to increasing the IMF lending capacity at the IMF and World Bank meeting in Toronto in September 1982 and continued American pursuit of economic policy without regard to its effects on the rest of the world — bloody-minded unilateralism the *Financial Times* (11 December 1982) called it — gave way by the end of 1982 to world reality and a more pragmatically universalist American realism. In the face of the very real threat of total world economic collapse, the American administration opted for a perhaps last attempt to lead its allies to hang together economically on pain of hanging separately if the financial trap door under them crashes open.

West-West Conflict over North-South Trade

Transatlantic conflicts of interest and policy over international trade and foreign policy issues have increasingly shaped the North-South debates and negotiations in which the Americans and Europeans appear as competitors as often as allies. Through the late 1970s the Americans were joined and sometimes even outdone by the Germans in their hard line opposition to any concessions to Third World demands for a New International Economic Order (NIEO) at the many conferences and negotiations at the World Bank and International Monetary Fund and the 1977 International Finance conference in Jamaica; the United Nations, UNCTAD, FAO and Law of the Sea conferences; the Paris North-South Dialogue; and elsewhere. The smaller European countries and especially the Scandinavian ones and Holland always were more conciliatory to Third World demands for bending or (as the recalcitrant opponents claimed) abrogating the sacred law of the market, in which the smaller European industries and countries also found themselves at a disadvantage second only to the Third World. More recently, however, Germany has also softened its line towards the Third World, and the American government has sought to impose its Reaganomic marketeering on the South almost alone, except for the loyal political support of Mrs Thatcher's Britain, while the Third World view has found its loudest northern echo in Mitterrand's Socialist Party government of France (which has not hesitated to continue pushing its arms exports to the Third World right behind the US and the USSR). For instance, the US unilaterally torpedoed the laboriously negotiated compromise on the UN Law of the Sea and dragged its feet alone on Global Negotiations (the new euphemism for the illfated NIEO) until Canada and France in particular elicited a grudging provisional go-ahead for talks from Reagan only in return for concessions to the Americans' hard line on financial matters at the summits in Cancun, Mexico and Versailles.

The developments underlying these shifts in interest and policy seem to be that the Europeans have become much more competitive and competition minded on Third World markets. An early manifestation of this development was the German proposal to sell nuclear power plants and fuels to Brazil and the French one to Pakistan in a very depressed international market on which the United States and the Soviet Union had previously had a virtual monopoly. The Americans immediately raised a storm of protest against the dangers of nuclear proliferation to Third World powers that might convert this technology and material into atomic bombs. In the meantime, the much more threatening development of the bomb by Israel and South Africa proceeded much more quietly, while the Brazilian and Pakistani projects were put on ice under American pressure.

European and American competition also noticeably increased in each others' economic backyards and political spheres of interest in the Third World. The Europeans and the Japanese increased their penetration of traditionally US markets in Latin America in everything from automobiles, equipment and machinery, to agricultural products. The Third World magazine *SOUTH* (February 1982) reported that the EEC "is planning closer trade and economic links with Central America, including a co-operation agreement and increased financial assistance for eight states". This initiative is backed by France and Germany, but "the United States will consider any 'special relationship' with these eight states an intrusion into its own sphere of influence. There has been speculation that the US may retaliate by making inroads into the southern Mediterranean states, the EEC's 'backyard'." The political accompaniment to this eagerly pursued incipient and fervently hoped for penetration of previously private American economic hunting preserves has been the increasingly vocal overtures and political economic support of social democratic Second International parties and even armed political movements in Latin America by European and especially German social democracy, under the leadership of Willy Brandt, while the Americans back the military dictatorships and at best Christian Democratic civilian alternatives in Latin America. The resulting political conflict became most visible through European social democratic support for the Sandinista movement and then government in Nicaragua and for the opposition to the American backed government in El Salvador. Ironically (but as we may observe in the review of East-West relations below not so uncharacteristically) the Reagan administration White Paper on El Salvador in early 1981 called the opposition a typically Soviet communist plot when the Soviet Union or Cuba had sent no material support to the rebels but the West German Social Democrats had! The French competed with the US for Mexican oil while it was still scarce and then underlined the continuing transatlantic conflict of interest and policy over Central America by selling arms to the Sandinista government in Nicaragua.

Only over the war in the Falkland/Malvinas Islands have the Americans and Europeans lined up on the same side with Britain, though the West Germans have done so very halfheartedly to protect their NATO interests and collaboration with Britain, while the French Socialist Government has lent Britain its fullest support, possibly with a view to receiving the same when her own remaining colonial possessions may be threatened.

The opposite is happening in Africa, where the Americans seek to penetrate French and British markets, inherited from the latter's colonial empires and then consecrated through the Lome Convention between the EEC and the ACP (Africa, Caribbean, Pacific) countries, which inevitably also opened the door to West Germany. This treaty provides for preferential trade and some price support for trade between ACP countries and the EEC. United States policy is trying to mobilise opposition to the Lome Convention amongst the countries who are supposedly discriminated against through their exclusion from this arrangement by virtue of their not having been British or French colonies! The US is also encouraging ACP objections to EEC extension of trade agreements to non-member states in Central America. The *New York Times* (7 March, 1982) quotes David Rockefeller as recently telling Africans that his Chase Manhattan Bank "has found that we can deal with almost any kind of government as long as it is methodical and responsible . . .

The more African countries I see who call themselves Marxist, the more it seems to me that this is a matter of labels and ornaments, and not of realities'', adding that therefore he does not regard African Marxism to be a threat to the United States or to the interests of its firms (retranslated from the Spanish in *Comercio Exterior*, May 1982). At the same time, the United States is courting the still predominantly British South Africa for its raw materials, lucrative market and strategic position.

East Asia and increasingly Australia has been left substantially to Japan and India to the Soviet Union, but both the Americans and the Europeans are making some efforts to reassert their economic and political influence in the region generally and especially in and in part through China. However, the more Japan is excluded by European or American competition elsewhere the greater will its dependence be on Asia. There is a possible revival of the Japanese "Greater East Asian Co-Prosperity Sphere" of the 1930s through the creation of a new Japan-Asia bloc in the 1980s or 1990s. The possible collaboration by China and the United States in a Pacific Basin and Rim strategy remains to be seen.

The main bone of contention between the Americans and Europeans, however, is the Middle East. Europe is highly dependent on oil imports from the Middle East and on exports to pay for them. Exports to the Middle East OPEC countries and the Socialist countries provided an essential safety net for the West, and especially for European heavy industry during the slump of Western demand in the 1973-75 recession and its subsequent faltering recovery. The inability of both market areas to pay for similar imports and increases of Western exports during the 1979-1982 recession is a major reason for the failure of the European economies, which are much more dependent on them than the American, to weather the last recession as well as the previous one. Moreover, although the Europeans have a payments surplus with the Socialist and non-oil exporting Third World countries, the Europeans have a significant trade and payments deficit with the

USA, Japan and of course OPEC. In view of the already reviewed trilateral conflict among the industrial capitalist regions of the West, it is all the more important for Europe to redress its deficit with the Middle East as much as possible by exporting there in return — and driving the Americans and Japanese out of these lucrative markets. This is the economic background for the European political disagreements with the United States about foreign policy with regard to Iran and the American embargo sparked by the US Tehran embassy "hostage" crisis as well as with regard to the Israeli-Arab conflict and especially the Palestine issue. The Americans sponsored the Camp David accords between Israel and Egypt, for which the latter was isolated by other Arabs as a traitor to their cause. The Europeans, especially at their 1980 declaration in Venice, instead lent some support to the PLO and the formation of a separate Palestinian state (which are anathema to the Begin government in Israel, but are contemplated by its Peres Labour Party, and recommended by far-sighted Americans such as the former Under-Secretary of State, George Ball, who tirelessly insists that a settlement of the Israeli-Arab conflict and the Palestine issue on terms more favourable to the latter is essential to guard American interests in what he and others regard as the focal point of Western interests).

In this context, it is revealing that the above cited four Western foreign policy institutes recognise this West-West conflict of interests and write in their chapter on "The Security Situation in the Third World":

> "We can also agree to take a relatively relaxed view about a number of so-called 'Marxist' regimes in the Third World whose relationship with the Soviet Union is tenuous and cynical. Speaking merely in ideological terms, the Soviet drive in the Third World has been unsuccessful . . . and there are many countries whose political label as such does not hurt Western interests . . .
>
> "*Where Western interests are at stake, Europe and the United States should agree on the need for a Western capacity to intervene and should take steps to improve their capacity for doing so . . .*
>
> "At present the main region in the category is that of the Middle East and the Gulf . . . The threats to this supply [of oil] come from

> four main directions: *The menace of Soviet military power* . . . *National and ethnic rivalries* . . . *Revolution or internal disruption* . . . *A new Arab-Israeli war* . . . The failure to solve the Palestinian problem is a permanent contribution to the instability of the whole area . . .
>
> "These considerations point to active European military participation on the ground and at sea in the Middle East . . . [and] *the main burden of putting together a rapid deployment force falls on the United States, but the Europeans make some contribution in terms of men and material*" (pp.35-38, all emphasis in the original).

To organise the same, the report proposes seven-nation summits "devoted at least as much to political and security concerns as to economic ones" and the formation of "principal nations groups . . . [for] crisis management and joint assessments". "The first such group to be formed immediately should be on the Gulf/South West Asian region" (pp.44-48). Nonetheless in the face of a new Arab-Israeli war, timed by the latter's invasion of Lebanon to coincide with the Versailles economic and Bonn NATO summit meetings in June 1982, the assembled leaders of the West failed even to agree on a joint NATO statement, let alone action, to respond to the occasion, as the *Financial Times* (11 June, 1982) observed in its editorial. But the European heads of state assembled at an EEC summit a couple of weeks later issued a joint communique demanding Israeli withdrawal from Lebanon, although without even hinting at an embargo on Israel, such as they imposed on Argentina over the conflict with Britain.

Western Conflicts over East-West Trade

Soviet armed intervention in Afghanistan in December 1979 is widely claimed to have undermined the East-West detente of the 1970s and to have ushered in the beginnings of a new cold war. But the Soviet Union had reason to believe that detente and especially its relations with the United States were deteriorating anyway, independently of Soviet policy: it had after all offered to defuse tension in Europe by pulling some of its troops out of East Germany. The United States to the contrary had in fact been blowing an increasingly cold war wind in the Soviet face for some time. The US Senate had been dragging its feet against ratifying the SALT II arms control treaty, so laboriously negotiated in good faith by the USSR with the US, while the latter was preparing and then announced a new programme to install intercontinental MX missiles in its Western states (whose vulnerability would only make them adequate for first strike purposes). To add insult to injury, the US increasingly used its "China card" against the Soviet Union. The Carter administration also pledged to increase real military expenditure by 3 per cent per year and elicited promises from its NATO partners to do the same (in an economic climate in which consumer, investment and export demand were unstable or lagging). Most significantly, NATO had already taken its "Two Track" decision to install new Pershing and Cruise missiles directed toward the Soviet Union from European soil by 1983 and in the meantime to use this track and threat to provide strength to the US to negotiate a new arms control agreement with the Soviet Union on another track, that Carter's successor Reagan would baptise START. That is, the US Carter administration had been blowing very cool air on detente already before the events in Afghanistan, which the US then used to justify even colder blows (and Carter himself used to take the wind out of the Kennedy challenge to his Democratic nomination) before Reagan defeated him and made the cold war wind even icier.

The new Reagan administration, in the throes of a nostalgia to make America No.1 again, certainly developed what the four foreign policy institutes termed "the tendency to consider every event in the world in purely East-West terms" to the nth degree. Among other things, it immediately set out to dispatch Carter's modest 3 per cent annual increase of military expenditures to the garbage heap and to escalate the arms race several fold. Apart from the hoped for salutary economic effects of arms spending in the United States (which Reagan soon found to be dampened by their unsalutary effects on the budget deficit and Congress) the *Washington Post* editorialised, "there is a crucial economic dimension to the Reagan strategy for dealing with Soviet power. It is that the Soviet Union, although a superpower, is relatively backward and cannot keep up in arms-building competition without suffering even harsher internal strains. This has been, of course, a familiar element in Western thinking about the Soviet Union since 1917 . . . It is being asked now, however, whether this time around the Soviet Union may not be near a bending point — some observers say a breaking point — after all" (*International Herald Tribune*, 19 November, 1981).

On the occasion of the dispute about the gas pipeline, the US Ambassador to France officially clarified: "I welcome this opportunity to explain our actions. This is the background: The Soviet economy is in trouble . . . One is a serious shortage of [foreign] currency in relation to ambitious five-year plans . . . Their foreign cash flow is down because of a drop in prices of oil" etc., and the United States wants to keep it down. The Ambassador goes on to explain that

> "I do not see the pipeline issue as primarily one of European dependence . . . The central point is that the Russians are in economic trouble . . . [and] the United States is perfectly justified in refusing actively to facilitate the quantum leap forward that will come from the Russians' expanded use of gas . . . [of which] 85 per cent is to be used to fuel Soviet internal industry . . . [and] provide the basis for further industrial expansion, which would otherwise be impossible . . . [and which] would have a profound beneficial effect on Soviet industrial, and subsequently Soviet military, capability . . . This view is the primary basis of the American measures against the Siberian pipeline" (*International Herald Tribune* 24-25 July, 1982).

Of course, this new American economic offensive strategy against the Soviet Union also includes other moves. The Carter administration had used the Afghanistan issue to impose a grain embargo against the Soviet Union, which was broken by the Argentine military junta and never totally enforced even in North America and which the far right Republican candidate Reagan promised to annul, which he finally did. The US also lengthened the list of prohibited "strategic" exports to the Soviet Union. The Americans boycotted the Moscow Olympics in the summer of 1980 and twisted as many allied arms as possible to do the same – with varying success in Europe in the face of their allies' responses, which varied from recalcitrance to grudging support (except from Mrs Thatcher, whose British athletes went to Moscow anyway). More seriously, the United States started trying to infuse the cold war Co-Com(mittee) with new life to procure agreement from its NATO allies to increase the list of industrial items whose export or licensing to the Soviet Union is embargoed for "strategic" reasons. Since exports to the Soviet Union and Eastern Europe – except for grain – are small potatoes to the United States, it could well afford to press for such export prohibition. Its implementation would however impose a significant absolute loss of markets, profits and jobs on some European economies, and thereby help to weaken them relative to the United States to boot. Exports to the East account for 6 per cent of Western Europe and for 6 to 9 per cent of the exports and 1.5 per cent of the GNP of West Germany. But several hundred thousand jobs and untold profits depend directly on these exports from Germany and France and a small number of very large heavy industrial equipment firms and their banking connections would face serious losses from the reduction of trade with the Soviet Union and Eastern Europe. Some medium sized German companies depend for 30 to 40 per cent of their trade with the East and would face bankruptcy by its elimination. Not surprisingly, therefore, the Europeans have steadfastly rejected most of the American proposals and the hypocrisy of their political justification in the face of renewed US grain exports to the Soviet Union. The American "red alert" about technology transfer with subsidised credit to the Soviet Union and Eastern Europe awoke some Europeans but failed to move them.

This increasingly serious conflict of economic interest and acrimonious political disagreement over foreign policy came to a head over the crisis, martial law declaration, and debt management in Poland. The Americans sought to blame all of the events in Poland on the Soviet Union and to cut off trade and credits to both of them as much as possible. The American Secretary of Defence Weinberger even went so far as to propose that the West refuse all further credit rollover or refinancing of the US$27 billion Polish debt in order to force Poland into default and to oblige the Soviet Union to pick up the pieces and carry the burden. Secretary of State Haig replied that a Polish default "could bring the ruin of East-West trade and mean the collapse of the West German economy" and other far-reaching and unpredictable effects and that "had we followed the advice of some, we'd be in a hole . . . [and] have the Europeans side with the Russians" (*Guardian*, 20 February, 1982). Wiser counsels in the Department of State and among virtually all Europeans involved prevailed to quash the Weinberger idea, whose implementation would also have seriously exposed several major European banks to failure and thereby threatened to start a chain reaction throughout the entire Western banking system, which could bring its already exceedingly unstable financial house of cards crashing down. Already before the 13th of December, 1981, the *Financial Times* (22 June, 1981) quoted the explanation of an international banker: "In essence the problem is simple. They've got our money and can't repay: either we agree to wait, or we write it off. With so much money at stake no one wants to take the loss. So we agree to wait — we have no choice". The declaration of martial law and military rule in Poland — as an alternative to Soviet intervention — in no wise increased the range of choice. Rather the contrary, it undermined the "umbrella" theory according to which the Soviet Union would eventually (especially after any Soviet military intervention) be willing or obliged — as a sort of lender of last resort — to bail Poland and other East European debtor countries out of their inability to pay. Soviet inaction in this regard left the entire East European trade and financial situation temporarily a bit confused.

In 1981, West Germany's trade with the East went into deficit for the first time as the economic and debt crisis in East and West undermined business. Then the Polish crisis was followed soon after by Romania's inability to service her debt, which also had to be rescheduled. Western bankers suffered a severe crisis of confidence in Eastern Europe's formerly good as gold ability to pay and in the supposed umbrella insurance of Soviet gold as a last resort. Suddenly all of Eastern Europe suffered a liquidity crisis, as even the miracle economies of Hungary and East Germany found themselves unable to raise syndicated loans through regular Western financial channels (which also observed that precisely these two countries already have the highest debt/population or GNP ratios). German industrialists feared that the fat years of sustained East-West trade expansion were over, and bankers sought to avoid any further unnecessary risks (*Der Spiegel* No.5, 1982). Both inclined to lend a more attentive ear than before to the American advocacy of economic sanctions against the East. But only with uncertainty.

The *Business International* newsletter for multinational executives advised its readers that "the US-USSR face-off over martial law in Poland will sorely test the Atlantic Community, already severely taxed by several other strains. Europeans felt that many headaches are being thrust upon them by the US: high interest rates, recession, nuclear weaponry and now, economic sanctions against the USSR" (8 January, 1982) and examined "Beyond Poland: Broader Implications for World Business . . . Delay for Western European recovery . . . Disruption of East-West trade . . . The Soviet-West European pipeline . . . Further energy distortions . . . The debt debacle . . . Soviet burden" to keep Poland afloat (18 December, 1981).

Other headlines in *Business International* (BI) and its affiliates *Business Europe* (BE) and *Business Eastern Europe* (BEE) in early and mid-1982 were revealing:

"Confusion Follows Reagan Trade Ban" (BEE 25 June, 1982); "Summits Underline Soviet Role in Trade" (BEE 18 June); "Trade War Threat to US Exports" (BE 18 June); "US Business opposes

Reagan Sanctions" (BEE 26 February); "Western Imports Vital to Polish Economy" (BEE 19 February).

Confirmation of the last one came from the Polish Deputy Minister of Foreign Trade (quoted by the *Financial Times* 26 March 1982): "We must realise that demands that our imports from the West be replaced by imports from the Socialist countries is out of tune with economic reality. For the moment such large scale changes are not possible". At the same time, the size and membership of the West German official business and government delegations to the Leipzig Trade Fair in East Germany led the *Financial Times* (22 March, 1982) to observe that "there appears to be no drop in West German interest to revive East-West trade which, it is hoped, is only temporarily in the doldrums" and West German Chancellor "Schmidt opposes Soviet trade war . . . Despite concern over the US attitude, the West German government feels all European Community countries are agreed in their desire to avoid a trade war with the East" (*Financial Times* 1 April, 1982). On 31 May the *International Herald Tribune* observed that Eastern Europe's creditworthiness was again starting to improve, and since then Hungary and Romania have received new credits while Poland's balance of trade registered significant improvements.

As a counter to European resistance to sanctions over Poland and to their objections to Cocom reclassification of items for export embargo, the Americans tried another tack: the reclassification of the countries in the East into the richer country categories, which do not merit concessional credit terms or guarantees for suppliers from Western governments. The European governments have again resisted the American pressures, while individual firms and/or their banks have been absorbing the difference between the officially supported interest rates on supplier credits and the even lower real interest that they charge Eastern buyers under the table to secure the contracts. The United States pressed its allies on this matter at the Versailles summit and received a grudging but vague commitment from them which led to an agreement a few weeks later to reclassify the credit eligibility of all countries and therefore to increase the official credit costs to the East (until interest rates fall).

Another issue of East-West trade that brought Europe into conflict with the United States is the construction and finance of the gas pipeline and the export of gas from the Soviet Union through Eastern Europe to Western Europe. The Americans have claimed to be concerned that Western European dependence on some energy from the Soviet Union would endanger the security of the West Europeans, who do not share this concern or even believe the concern of the Americans, who have offered to sell Europe surplus American coal instead! The Europeans argue that they plan to derive only a small part of about 6 per cent of their energy supplies from the Soviet Union, in fact reducing European dependence on Middle Eastern oil, and that the construction of the pipeline provides much needed outlets for European steel and equipment. Moreover the eventual Western European purchase of more Soviet gas will provide the Soviet Union with a steady stream of hard currency with which to buy industrial and agricultural imports from the West, from which Europe of course hopes to benefit more than the United States. The Americans argue that "we" cannot afford to underwrite Soviet economic development with Western business finance and government guarantees; while the Europeans argue that they cannot afford not to guarantee their own economic growth through business with the East. In other terms, while an American Senator argues that the US should pull its troops out of Europe if Europeans insist on "business and life as usual" with the East, the French Minister of Trade replied to the American emissary sent to plead for credit restrictions against the East that "our principle is that trade is life. If you don't have trade you could have, as the end result, war" (*Guardian*, 4 March, 1982).

The gas pipeline issue, after building up in combination with American pressure on Europe to restrict export credits to the East and the US decision to impose countervailing duties on European steel, suddenly brought on American and European political explosions after the June 1982 Versailles summit (and after the bulk of this essay was written). The summit had produced an uneasy compromise involving European acceptance of some (undefined) concessions on export credits and American ones on the gas pipeline. A week later, apparent shifts in the balance of power within the Reagan administration led the President of the United States to order the prohibition of pipeline component deliveries also by extra-territorial holders of US licences for technology in Europe and elsewhere. Secretary of State Alexander Haig resigned in protest against this decision (which was taken in his absence against his known opposition to it) and others including support for Israel after the invasion of Lebanon, over which he was in conflict with Secretary of Defence Weinberger and National Security Advisor Clark. The political wisdom of both the American pipeline decision and US support for Israel in Lebanon was editorially questioned by the *New York Times* and the *Washington Post*. The shaky legality of "Reagan's March Toward Economic War" through American prohibitions to non-American firms on foreign soil was highly questioned even in the US, and the Europeans threatened to take the matter to the International Court of Justice.

The European reaction was unprecedented in post-war history. The EEC Commission demanded that the US rescind its pipeline decision. The EEC foreign ministers "denounced US actions in firm and menacing terms"; the EEC heads of state summit meeting issued a joint declaration against the US decision and also called for the withdrawal from Lebanon of Israel, which enjoys US support. The Vice-President and Industry Commissioner of the EEC declared "we are in a state of extreme political and economic tension with Washington" (*International Herald Tribune*, 23 June 1982).

National protests in Germany, France, Britain, Japan and elsewhere were even stronger. The governing Social Democratic Party in Germany accused the US of "interference in internal European affairs" and the German Finance Minister of failing to observe the sovereignty of other states, which would seriously affect the credibility of US companies abroad; the head of the German industrial association predicted major new tensions between Europe and America; the head of Germany's biggest union referred to American "insolence"; and Chancellor Helmut Schmidt announced that the pipeline and gas deal would proceed as contracted. The already tottering German electric industry giant AEG faced immediate bankruptcy if its AEG-Kanis division were unable to proceed with its gas-turbine deliveries order, which is worth about $300 million. A number of French and Italian firms were also liable to suffer severely (*Financial Times* 21, 22, 24, 28 June 1982). French President Mitterrand, who has lent Reagan's political anti-Soviet line substantial support, "delivered a wide-ranging attack on US economic and financial policy" and his government prepared for an "uncompromising fight against the US decision". The Japanese Premier Suzuki and his International Trade and Industry Minister also protested and asked for exemption of the offshore Siberian Sakhalin gas project, in which Japan has a direct interest. The British Minister of Trade denounced "an attempt to export unemployment from the US to Europe", and President Reagan's most faithful ally and anti-Soviet ideologue, Prime Minister Thatcher announced in Parliament that any British firm that observed this American ruling would be violating British law and would be prohibited by her government from complying with the American prohibition to sell to the Soviet Union! (*Financial Times* 29 and 30 June and 1 July). The Italian government concretely signified its rejection of the Reagan decision by having its state-owned engineering company supply turbines for the pipeline in fulfilment of its contract despite the American prohibition to do so (*Financial Times*, 8 July, 1982). Then, all of these major European governments declared that the American pipeline ban should be defied and that their firms would fulfil their delivery contract.

The newly named EEC ambassador to Washington declared in response to all this that "our trade relations with the United States are the worst I have seen since the end of the war . . . [and] I am not excluding that the situation with the [Reagan] administration will get worse" (*International Herald Tribune* 2 July, 1982). The situation did get worse throughout the summer and autumn of 1982 as the pipeline dispute became increasingly acrimonious until President Reagan was forced to backtrack in the face of united European opposition and increasing divisions within his own ranks. Reagan finally lifted the pipeline ban in return for a, for him, face saving but vague agreement by the Europeans to limit the list of exportable items and the state subsidised export credits to the Soviet Union and Eastern Europe that the Americans had long been demanding as observed above. Nonetheless, France hastened to deny that it had been party to any such agreement about East-West trade and that it rejects any "economic NATO" that might dictate allied commercial policy (*International Herald Tribune* 16 December 1982). However, no sooner was the pipeline dispute patched up than did European relations with the Reagan administration again take another turn for the worse over the threatened agricultural trade war and American demands at the November 1982 GATT ministerial conference and elsewhere that the Europeans reduce agricultural subsidies and protection. The problem is that each of these disputes about trade policy, no matter how it is papered over or resolved, is a recurrent manifestation of an inevitably deepening structural political economic conflict of interests between American and European capital and capitals.

NATO Alliance Conflicts over Strategic Issues

Paralleling these political economic conflicts over trade policy is the growing dispute over military expenditures and the stationing of new nuclear weapons in Europe with which the United States opened its new cold war offensive.

Anti-nuclear and peace movements throughout Western Europe (except France) and opposition parties especially in the parliaments of the smaller countries and Britain, but even strong opposition within the left wing of the Social Democratic Party in West Germany have rapidly grown in popular strength and in political influence. 200,000 to 400,000 people — a million within a single month — demonstrated against the stationing on their soil of new nuclear missiles in each of several countries. German Chancellor Helmut Schmidt told the United Nations that it is necessary to listen to these people who cannot all be wrong, but at home threatened to resign if they got their way. President Reagan and Secretary of State Haig first dismissed these European demonstrations of opposition to new American weapons as insignificant mass manipulations by Moscow and poured fuel on the fire of European fury and insecurity by declaring that Europe might become a theatre of nuclear war without direct American-Soviet nuclear engagement. The European response and the sudden development of a movement for local nuclear free zones and an arms freeze in the United States, however, obliged Reagan to alter his tactical stance. To take his own cold war wind out of the sails of these peace movement initiatives, Reagan proposed a "zero option" according to which the US offered to desist from placing the new missiles in Europe if the Soviet Union would dismantle or withdraw existing ones.

Moreover, political economic conflicts about strategic issues in East-West relations are weakening the NATO alliance itself as political disagreements grow wider and deeper between European and American allies and within Western Europe and the United States themselves. Debates have grown increasingly acrimonious about the burden of increasing military expenditures and the distribution of its shares, the related question of the costly stationing of American troops on European soil, the American proposal to increase NATO reliance on conventional weapons in Europe, and of course over the deployment of new generations of MX missiles in the US and cruise and Pershing II missiles in Europe as well as about the related Soviet-American negotiations on arms control.

The growing burden of military expenditures and their contributions to budget deficits have become increasingly onerous on both sides of the Atlantic and have fired up the long simmering trans-Atlantic dispute about "burden sharing". At a recent NATO ministers meeting, the British Secretary for Defence declared that none of the European members had any more money to spend on strengthened conventional forces beyond the 3 per cent annual increase they are already committed to (*Guardian*, 3 December 1982). American politicians and propagandists for their part are voicing louder and louder complaints that the Europeans are not paying enough for their own defence – and incidentally not buying enough American weapons for the same – and that if the ungrateful Europeans are not interested enough in their own defence to pay for it, the Americans should consider abandoning them to their fate and start by bringing the costly American troops home from Europe. "Is the US Congress an Ally of NATO?" asks a former US Under-Secretary of Defence in the *International Herald Tribune* (10 December 1982). He was commenting on Congressional proposals to cut American military spending in Europe, which "reflect a strain of neo-isolationism that is never far from the surface on Capitol Hill". The American NATO commander-in-chief, General Bernard Rogers, has poured further fuel on this debate through his recent "air-land battle" proposals to increase the absolute and relative reliance on new generations of highly accurate conventional weapons in Europe. Among the implications of this proposal are to increase the flexibility of response by the possibility of abandoning the forward defence or part of West Germany against any invading ground forces (which is politically unacceptable in Bonn), increasing European military expenditures for conventional weapons including American ones (which is politically unacceptable in most European capitals), and a looser relationship between the US and Europe (which is problematical if it is to be loosened on American terms).

American terms both to their European NATO allies and to the Soviet Union at the Geneva arms limitations talks have been turning on the proposals to deploy new generations of intercontinental MX missiles in the Western United States and of intermediate range cruise and Pershing II missiles in Western Europe. The December 1979 "Two Track" decision to threaten to place the latter missiles by the end of 1983 in five West European countries and in the meantime to use this threat as a bargaining counter in Soviet-American arms talks has fuelled the fires of the peace movement and the debates of the governments in Western Europe. Parliaments in Holland and Belgium have evidenced strong reluctance to the stationing of these new missiles on their soil. The Labour Party has rejected them for Britain. Even the most strongly Atlanticist French President Mitterrand has turned to ask for a solution somewhere between Reagan's zero option and the Soviet proposals. In West Germany, the environmental Greens have made political inroads on this issue, which has also split the Social Democratic Party. Christian Democrat commitment to go ahead with the missile placement was a major issue in the March 1983 elections not only for the Germans but for the Soviet-American arms negotiations in Geneva, since firm German government commitment to the missile placement is essential for the strength of the US negotiating position in Geneva. On the other hand, in the face of their own peace movements at home, West European government leaders must press the reluctant Americans to demonstrate serious negotiation of arms limitations in Geneva instead of playing for time until the new missiles can be installed on both sides of the Atlantic. This disagreement about approach also manifested itself with regard to the re-opening of the Helsinki conference in Madrid in late 1982, where the Americans wanted to pursue an intransigent tough line against the Soviet Union, while the Europeans insisted in using the Madrid conference to lay the basis for an East-West European security conference on "confidence building measures". However, challenges to the Reagan Administration military policy of build up and to its attempted justification through charges of Soviet military superiority, have also grown stronger in the United States itself. The nuclear freeze movement won referenda in nine states and several major cities, indeed everywhere that it was on the ballot except in Arizona, in the November 1982 elections. The House of Representatives voted down Reagan's "dense pack" MX missile siting proposal by a large majority. Reagan's military stance and propaganda have been publicly criticised by former President Carter and his ex-national security advisor Brzezinski, by former Secretaries of Defence McNamara and Schlesinger, and in less severe tones by Henry Kissinger, all of whom deny Reagan's supposed justification for his military policy. In a major article in *Newsweek* (29 November 1982) Kissinger also denies the supposed success of Soviet foreign policy (and notes that "it has been said, and not only as a joke, that the Soviet Union is the only country in the world entirely surrounded by hostile communist states") and observes that the war in Lebanon demonstrated the "near irrelevance of Soviet power in the Arab-Israeli conflict" and the near impotence of its tanks and planes in Syrian hands against those of Israel.

The Soviet Union for its part has repeatedly offered to withdraw missiles to beyond the Urals in return for some concessions and lesser threats from the Americans, and in June 1982 Brezhnev gave a Soviet pledge to the United Nations not to be the first to use nuclear weapons in the hope that the United States might make the same pledge, as proposed in an important *Foreign Affairs* article by McNamara, Bundy and others. In his subsequent United Nations speech, President Reagan failed to respond positively, while other American officials responded quite negatively. To commemorate the 60th anniversary of the founding of the Soviet Union, Brezhnev's successor, Yuri Andropov again offered to withdraw further Soviet SS-20 missiles from European soil and to reduce them to the number of British and French missiles in place.

This offer was followed in January 1983 by a Warsaw Pact proposal to NATO to sign a non-aggression pact, reminiscent of the Rapacki Plan of a quarter century earlier, which at the time was rejected by the West. The characteristically cool first response to both proposals by the United States was to call them "nothing new". The British and French disliked the first proposal to link arms reductions to their own stocks of nuclear weapons, which they like to regard as not part of NATO. But otherwise, the more forthcoming official responses, especially to the second proposal, in continental Europe and even in Britain, was to call the Soviet and Warsaw Pact proposals "worth studying". The reason for this difference in American and European responses is explained by the growing political strength of the peace movement in Europe, which is making insistence on the American "zero option" increasingly unrealistic. Thus, this new Soviet Peace offensive found an important echo in the European peace movement and served, perhaps designedly so, to drive the NATO allies farther apart on this issue as well.

In view of the consistently conciliatory Soviet stance on these nuclear issues and the fact, which is repeatedly emphasised in Washington, that the only Soviet strength lies in the military field since they are extremely and increasingly weak in the economic, political and ideological ones, the question arises why the West Europeans and Americans should consider the Soviet Union such a threat to their security. One answer is that according to opinion surveys, especially the younger generations in Europe no longer feel any such Soviet threat. The Americans continue to insist on it (although the youngest there also seem to feel more threatened by the bomb than by the Soviets).

Perhaps another answer to the question of the supposed threat by the Soviet Union is that not only it, but also the United States is increasingly economically and politically as well as ideologically weak relative to Western Europe, and that both superpowers can only rely on their nuclear arms and troops to exercise any decisive influence on and sway economic and trade policy in Western Europe! That is, in view of the shift in the economic and political balance of power from the United States to Europe, observed by their four foreign policy institutes, the only remaining ace in the American bargaining hand with the European powers is the American nuclear umbrella and the associated American troops on European soil that are supposed to make the American nuclear commitment to Europe credible. But of course, the United States can only maintain a nuclear ace up its sleeve if there *is* a corresponding Soviet threat against Europe from which the United States can protect — or threaten no longer to protect — the Europeans. Therefore, the Americans are obliged to and repeatedly do play up the Soviet nuclear and conventional arms threat to Western Europe for all it is worth. But it is worth less and less to more and more Europeans, especially as the Soviet Union is increasingly less able to keep its own and its East European neighbours' houses in economic and political order and could hardly be expected to intervene effectively let alone militarily in Western Europe. The real value of the supposed Soviet threat to Western Europe, which the Americans repeatedly try to conjure up by reference to and transference from real or supposed Soviet relations with Vietnam, the Middle East and Iran, Angola, Ethiopia, Afghanistan, Nicaragua and now El Salvador, is to the United States and its economic and political interests itself. For if Western Europeans once liberated themselves from the objectively unnecessary trauma of the supposed threat of a Russian bear embrace, the American bald eagle would find its wings very much clipped down to size. The American use of the nuclear ace to blackmail Western Europe (and Japan) on matters of conflicting economic and trade policy would become a useless joker, whose further attempted use by the Americans would render them ridiculous.

Chapter Two

Economic Crisis and Political Conflict in Eastern Europe

The Soviet Union and Eastern Europe also demonstrate "increasing participation . . . in the international division of labour, at levels and tempos normal for countries at their stage of economic development and fully in line with their economic strategies and plan objectives" (UN Economic Commission for Europe 1981: 6).

East-West trade, primarily with Western Europe, has consistently grown faster than intra-socialist trade since the death of Stalin in 1953. By the late 1970s trade with the West accounted for up to half of some East European countries' total foreign trade, although for Western Europe as whole exports to the East accounted for only 6 per cent of total exports. However, 30 per cent and 40 per cent annual increases of Western exports to the East, concentrated in machinery and agricultural products, during the 1973-75 recession provided an important safety net for falling intra-Western exports and deteriorating balances of payments after the oil price increase. During the 1975-79 recovery, Eastern exports to the West were able to increase again, albeit not as much as Eastern Europe had hoped for. During the 1979-82 recession western trade with the Soviet Union continued to grow, but trade with Eastern Europe failed to do so in view of the economic and political problems reviewed below. Nonetheless, the United Nations Economic Commission for Europe (1981: chapter 3, p.292) writes: "recent developments in the West have intensified western government and enterprise interest in maintaining, and if possible, even enlarging western exports to the east". This interest is also manifest in the continued increase in East-West intergovernmental economic and interfirm industrial co-operation agreements. Their number, which are concentrated in the metal using and machinery sectors, grew from 200 in 1971 to 600 in 1973 and over 1,000 in 1975; and they have continued to increase since then to include the major German, French and Italian 1981-82 agreements with the Soviet Union about pipeline construction and delivery for gas. The over 500 tripartite agreements, through which a western and an eastern enterprise collaborate in a third country, and especially in major Third World energy generating projects, have also continued to grow (details in Frank 1980 Chapter 4).

Especially in view of these growing East-West economic relations, the Soviet and East European economies have also been substantially affected by the world capitalist economic crisis, and their growth rates of output and productivity have declined for both internal reasons and those connected with their increasing integration into a crisis-ridden world economy (Frank 1980: Chapter 4). Growth rates of output and productivity fell noticeably during the 1976-1980 five year plan period, but their deceleration is part of a long term trend that appears to have begun a decade earlier. Annual growth rates of net material product declined in the Soviet Union from 7.8 per cent for 1966-70, to 5.7 per cent for 1971-75, to 4.2 per cent for 1976-80 and 3.2 per cent in 1981. In Eastern Europe the corresponding growth rates were 6.5 per cent for the first five year period, 7.8 per cent for the second in which Poland significantly elevated the rate and average, and 5.0 per cent for the last period, but excluding Poland whose absolute decline of output in 1979 would distort the average downward, and 2.8 per cent in 1981 excluding Poland or a decline of 1.3 per cent including Poland. Growth rates of labour productivity also declined during 1976-80 to rates often two-thirds and half or less those of 1971-75, and most spectacularly so in the Soviet Union where the overall average declined from 6 per cent to 3 per cent and in particular branches of industry from 5-7 per cent to 1 per cent and even lower. In nearly every case actual growth rates of output and productivity have been lower, and often significantly so, than planned rates for both plan periods in the 1970s and again in 1981. In the Soviet Union, no single output plan target was achieved in any year, and actual labour productivity in both industry and agriculture was barely half that planned. Yearly plan targets had to be repeatedly reduced when it became clear that they would not be achieved, which led Mr Brezhnev to complain about the further disorganisation of the economy through this procedure. Production of coal, steel, cement and agricultural commodities actually declined between 1977-78 and 1980 (*Economic and Political Weekly*, 5 December, 1981 and *Spiegel*, No.4, 1982). In the face of similar circumstances everywhere planned rates for 1981-85 in the Soviet Union and Eastern Europe have for the most part been significantly reduced even below the actual ones for 1976-80 (UNECE 1981 passim). Nonetheless, it already appears yet again that many of these plans will not be fulfilled during the present plan period.

> "A confidential study prepared for the Soviet leadership has outlined a near-disastrous decline in the Soviet Union's ability to feed itself . . . Figures showed a tenfold increase in Soviet imports over the past decade . . . For the period 1966 to 1970, the Soviet Union had to import 15 million tons of food, mainly grain and meat. From 1976 to 1980, food imports rose to 80 million tons . . . One-fifth of the grain harvest is lost because it is harvested too late or left to rot . . . One-third of the potato crop is left to rot . . . About half of potato production . . . is lost each year because of a chaotic distribution system and lack of storage facilities . . . The Commission . . . concluded that 'the existing economic mechanism does not provide necessary economic incentives for production increases and fuller use of the potentially available land'. The study has provided the basis for an internal debate leading to a special Central Committee meeting on agriculture, to be held Monday" (*International Herald Tribune*, 24 May, 1982).

A few days later, the press reported some of the decisions taken at this meeting in which President Brezhnev outlined "a new food programme: further encouragement of private plots and small-scale co-operative farming, significant decentralisation of the organisation of the farming system, and substantial new incentive payment schemes for farm managers and workers" (*Financial Times*, 27 May, 1982). However, new agricultural programmes and improved organisation have had to follow each other with alarming regularity since Khrushchev took over in 1953, and despite the large scale expansion, especially in Siberia, and the massive improvements West of the Urals, another reorganisation of agriculture is due now — and still another will be necessary again. For much of the problem of Soviet agriculture in fact must be traced to the inefficiency of Soviet industry and distribution as well: poor quality, shortages, and mal-distribution of spare parts, and the consequent perpetual breakdown of agricultural machinery places about half of it out of commission at each harvest time; and ploughing, sowing and fertilising for the next crop are further hampered by recurrent shortages of inputs from the industrial sector. Meat consumption in the Soviet Union has increased significantly over the past decade or more; but coincidentally as in Western Europe, much of the fodder for the livestock has had to be imported in the form of grain from North America, for which the Soviet Union is less and less able to afford the foreign exchange earned primarily through exports of fuel to Western Europe.

Another press report examines:

> "*The Soviet Economy, Why something has to give:* The Soviet economy has been sending out a series of unmistakable distress signals in the shape of forced sales of key hard-currency earners such as gold, diamonds, timber and oil products . . . It is also quietly running down its deposits with Western banks and borrowing more to pay for the Western equipment going into the Siberia-West Europe gas pipeline . . . What is more, the terms of trade have now also moved against the Soviet Union . . . On the other hand, the Soviet Union itself has reduced by 10 per cent, or 8m tonnes annually, the amount of oil it is prepared to sell to its Comecon partners on concessionary terms" (*Financial Times*, 5 February, 1982).

This development is one of several that also suggest that the Soviet Union finds it increasingly difficult if not impossible to continue supporting its allied economies in Eastern Europe through raw materials and prices that have risen significantly during the 1970s but still lag behind those on the world market. These circumstances, of course, place the economies of Eastern Europe in a scissors crisis: whilst import prices for raw materials from the Soviet Union to the East have risen, they suffer lower earnings from trade with the West due to inflated import prices for technology and reduced export prices and opportunities because of recession reduced demand in the West.

For Eastern Europe the result is imported inflation, reduced income, and an accumulation of debts to both the Soviet Union and the West. Between 1971 and 1981 the total Soviet Bloc debt to the West grew ten-fold from US$8 billion to $80 billion, of which $20 billion is owed by the large Soviet Union and $60 billion are owed by the small East European countries, of which $27 billion by Poland alone. "The economic crisis facing Eastern European countries has become so severe that governments have reached a turning point where leaderships must decide between reforms or a period of brutal austerity" (*International Herald Tribune*, 17 May, 1982). The background, briefly, is as follows.

In 1968-1970 far-reaching economic reforms were introduced in Hungary, which intentionally opened the economy to a large-scale trade with the West, linked the internal price system to that of the world market, extended and intensified the use of the market mechanism to income incentives, production and distribution, and permitted the development of a parallel grey market economy that is now estimated to account for over 30 per cent of Hungarian production and income. Though the economic reforms were slowed down again in the mid-1970s, they worked to increase income and consumer satisfaction without unduly offending the vital foreign sensibilities of the Soviet Union, whose staunch ally

Hungary remained within the Warsaw Pact and in international affairs.

Czechoslovakia also tried to introduce similar economic reforms through "socialism with a human face" in 1968, but failed to allay the fears of the Soviet Union, which invaded and quashed all of the reform initiatives. Under pressure of mass political revolt in 1969 and 1970, Poland also introduced some economic and agricultural reforms in 1970, and with spectacular success in terms of income, but reversed them again in the mid-1970s. Romania went on an industrialisation and industrial export drive but without any organisational reforms or an adequate agricultural infrastructure, which Bulgaria built up instead.

Beginning 1971-72 all of the East European countries (as well as the Soviet Union, China, and North Korea) almost simultaneously went on a concerted drive to import Western technology. They hoped to digest it economically, to use it to generate a surplus of industrial exports, and in the meantime to export raw materials to the West to pay for the imported technology. All of them miscalculated drastically, literally banking on continued Western prosperity: when this evaporated with the coming of the 1973-75 recession and the subsequent faltering 1975-79 recovery, not to mention the renewed 1979-82 recession, the economic rug was pulled out from under their calculations. Their import costs rose; their export possibilities shrank; their debts to finance the by then necessary component imports piled up; and then with sky-high Western interest rate, their costs to service this debt grew to the unsustainable proportions of often over 50 per cent — and for Poland over 100 per cent — of annual foreign exchange earnings.

So now "Eastern Europe has arrived at its moment of economic truth . . . The small East European countries — with the possible exception of Poland — have hardly any resources with which to pay off their massive . . . debt to the West . . . They are locked into a vicious circle of central planning commission issuing directives which soon become out of date, fictitious costs and prices, along with an economic structure which has been severely distorted over the past 37 years" (*Financial Times*, 9 February, 1982). In the 1970s, internal economic organisation and management – except in Hungary, although even it is beginning to feel the external crunch – have not been sufficiently flexible to permit adequate adaptation to the enormous technological, economic, social, cultural, political and ideological influences and changes imported from the West, not to mention the accumulated indigenous problems and their strained economic relations with the Soviet Union. The question arises whether the East European economies have reached or even passed the point of no return in this headlong plunge into extensive external economic relations with the West without concomitant internal reorganisation and intensive domestic growth. Now the East European economies certainly must reorganise their economies internally.

But there is also increasing evidence that the East European and to a lesser extent Soviet economies have indeed passed this point of no return and that only a flight forward to further integration and not a renewed involution is economically and politically possible. Beyond their now already built-in economic dependence on the West – illustrated by the above quoted observation by the Polish Deputy Minister of Foreign Trade that replacing imports from the West by others from the Socialist countries is for the moment out of tune with reality – there are internal economic constraints that are connected to this externally related reality. In general, the slowdown in growth and productivity in the Soviet Union and Eastern Europe can be traced to the growing maturity of their economies, the increasing scarcity and costliness both domestically and internationally of material inputs and the growing scarcity of labour as demographic changes and reduced rural-urban migration militate against supply constrained growth; the difficulties, often bordering on impossibility, of making the transition from mobilising resources for extensive growth to increasing their productivity for intensive growth; the rigidity of economic planning, organisation and incentive motivation that militate against technological change; the simultaneous opening of their economies to technological imports, exports and world market prices to overcome this limitation externally and the increasingly far-reaching privatisation of economic incentives, rewards and decisions in a more extensive market economy internally.

The turning point to reforms or brutal austerity, or more likely a mixture of both has been brought on by the moment of economic truth in the most dramatic way in Poland. Spectacular rates of economic growth and income through the mid-1970s, brought on in large part through the opening to the West and partly through internal agricultural reform, turned out to be unsustainable, especially without accompanying organisational reform of the economy and continuation of the agricultural reform. Growth slowed down again after the mid-1970s, and in 1979 total output actually fell by 2 per cent. In 1980 the drop in output accelerated to 4 per cent and obliged the government to impose austerity measures, (already attempted in 1976 but retracted in the face of popular unrest), which included the increases in the price of meat that sparked off the strike wave that began in August 1980 and developed into the 10 million strong Solidarity movement. In 1981, output declined a massive 14 per cent, only secondarily as a result of Solidarity work stoppages and disorganisation, and primarily because of shortages of domestic and foreign inputs derived from the malfunctioning of the economy in general. Further austerity measures were demanded by the West (banks, IMF, etc.), the Soviets, and the Polish government but were politically unenforceable. These economic and political problems led to the imposition of martial law on 13 December, 1981. Solidarity has been legally supressed, interest payment on the Polish debt has been rescheduled despite Western reservations and arguments for sanctions, imports have been drastically reduced, output especially of foreign exchange earning coal has been revived; and according to a spokesman for the new military government the sweeping price rises, often tripling and quadrupling the prices of basic necessities, were the start of the "biggest upheaval in post-war history of a socialist country" whose economic reforms would now go further even than those of Hungary. (*Financial Times*, 2 February, 1982.) Soon Poland began to cut state subsidised bank credits to enterprises making losses and to permit or even encourage the unemployment of workers.

However, the same day's press also reports "Czechs stunned by steepest food price rises in 30 years . . . [and] the authorities are preparing for other austerity measures . . . and the official media have launched a campaign to explain that without price increases and other savings, the country would find itself heading for a catastrophic financial crisis". (*Financial Times*, 2 February, 1982). In Hungary itself, where income declined by 1 per cent and investment by 8 per cent, an economist member of the Party Central Committee observed that "continuation of reforms is not just an alternative as it was in 1968. It is . . . a necessity"; and the head of the Hungarian Institute for World Economics observes that "we have been running too egalitarian a wage and salary system . . . We must increase the flexibility of the Hungarian economy and introduce more incentives", including the sale to private entrepreneurs of state-owned restaurants and small shops, and of course some ways to finance the foreign debt, which relative to the size of the economy is Eastern Europe's highest, at a time when Hungary's balance of payments is seriously deteriorating (*International Herald Tribune*, 27 and 14 May, 1982). The other highest per capita debt economy, East Germany, demonstrated substantial strength and development during the 1970s, but has not escaped the world, Western, East European, and Soviet (to which it supplies industrial products whose makeup is to be changed) economies' several and common economic crises. Romania still resists economic reforms, which the government may feel are still too dangerous to introduce while its head is physically assaulted by angry mobs in the streets and factories; but it must nonetheless impose severe austerity measures in the face of the near bankruptcy of its economy and its intermittent incapacity to pay even the interest on its foreign debt in response to which the IMF, of which Romania is a member, has recommended its usual belt-tightening remedies. The continued success of agriculture in Bulgaria (as in Hungary and East Germany) absolves it of similar belt-tightening, but not from the introduction of a "new economic mechanism" to achieve greater cost-effectiveness.

The political events in Poland and the foreign debt crisis there and in Romania produced a short run setback to East-West political detente (or at least to West German and European efforts to safeguard it) as the Americans pressed for "sanctions" and to the further extension of Western credits to Eastern Europe as the banks came to fear for the safety of their money. In Eastern Europe and particularly Poland and Romania themselves an initial reaction also was to look to Comecon for more economic ties and to turn to the Soviet Union for more political support. However, there are important economic and political reasons why this East European step backwards toward political economic involution may be a short one and why these events, paradoxically, could lay the basis for a longer term further flight forward to more extensive political economic ties between Eastern Europe and the West. For such an involution would further increase the Soviet economic burden and political responsibility of supporting the East European austerity measures and their political unpopularity in the supply-constrained Comecon economies. Paradoxically, the political economic crisis of Poland could pave the way for more stable long term economic relations with Western Europe and especially Germany, which could help ease the Soviet and East European supply constraints, reduce their need for austerity and therefore permit greater political liberalisation, while at the same time combating Western Europe's own demand and cost constraints.

In the face of this deepening economic crisis in Eastern

Europe and the economic and political transformations occurring and impending in each of the countries, in their relations to each other, and in their relations to both the Soviet Union and the West, the political room for manoeuvre or margin of choice may often be tight and/or the problem of timing may be delicate. However, this room could be enlarged and the time lengthened through appropriate political economic relations with both the Soviet Union and Western Europe, which could be in the interest of important economic interests and influential political forces in each of these three regions. Smoother progress of economic reforms, and a minimisation of austerity in Eastern Europe, as well as a reduction of the economic burden or responsibility for the Soviet Union could be in the interest of many interest groups in these countries themselves — and in Western Europe also. Such a decline in the economic burden to the Soviet Union and of the burden of austerity in Eastern Europe itself could be facilitated through appropriate economic — and political — co-operation between Western and Eastern Europe, or even a sort of West European "Marshall Plan" in Eastern Europe, such as was proposed for Poland from someone in its Foreign Trade Ministry after martial law (*Financial Times*, 3 April, 1982). For a Western European economy beset by low profiles and high unemployment in industry as well as by agricultural surpluses, such an arrangement could offer some attraction to influential economic and political interest groups. The important underlying political economic opportunities for both Eastern and Western Europe through the export of western agricultural surpluses to the East have been highlighted by the recurrent Soviet "great grain robbery" from the United States and President Reagan's offer of increased grain sales to the Soviet Union during his pipeline ban, as well as by the West European "butter mountain" and the political pressures surrounding its subsidised sale to the East, where these purchases help relieve economic and social tensions. *Business International* (12 February, 1982) and its division *Business Eastern Europe* (21 May,

1982) look forward to the next five years of "prospects for profits [in] Comecon" by emphasising "planning chaos, energy/agriculture key, creative financing needed" and observe that the Soviet Union and Poland have "left Comecon countries convinced that they must strive for economic independence . . . and greater emphasis in each member nation on developing its own industrial sectors in competition with those of its bloc trading partners . . . (and plant managers) greater freedom to make both import and export decisions . . . Western firms will want to take note of this" and keep or develop their sales organisations in Eastern Europe accordingly. But perhaps the very crisis in Eastern and Western Europe can generate conditions for joint "creative financing" of their crisis management strategies beyond those of Western firms and embrace their associated banks and states to a greater extent than they already do.

Commenting on the succession of Yuri Andropov to leadership in the Kremlin, the Western press frequently noted that since his days as Soviet Ambassador to Budapest during the intervention in 1956, he has maintained a special expertise in East European affairs and lent strong support to the Hungarian economic reforms. At the same time, the press also observed that Andropov's first major speech as Premier was on the need for economic reform in the Soviet Union, that "thus, to forestall further unrest at a time when he is facing major problems at home, Mr Andropov may be willing to tolerate a greater degree of economic experimentation and reform in Eastern Europe, as long as this remains carefully circumscribed and controlled by the party" as in Hungary (*International Herald Tribune* 10 December 1982) and that "the counterpart to greater assertion by Moscow of Soviet economic interests is greater freedom for its allies to work out their own economic salvation" (*Financial Times* 24 November 1982). These possibilities may offer new political economic policy alternatives in both Eastern and Western Europe.

Chapter Three

Political Economic Alternatives

Striving for economic independence and the greater emphasis on national industrial developments are, of course, not limited to Eastern Europe, but are important tendencies in the West on both sides of the Atlantic. In the West, however, these defensive economic and offensive political nationalist tendencies will appear less profitable and thus less welcome to important sectors especially of multinational business. Instead, this resurgent political economic nationalism appeals to and is furthered by strange bedfellows from the right and the left of the political spectrum. Such *de facto* political agreement on economic nationalism is clearly visible, for instance, in France and Britain. In France, the nationalism of the Gaullists now led by Jacques Chirac is rivalled – or perhaps even excelled – only by the Communists "à la couleur de France" led by George Marchais, although one of the main planks in the Socialist economic programme of President Mitterrand also is "to reconquer the French market" for French industry. In Britain, the proposal to abandon the Common Market has become official Labour Party policy after having long been the flag of the nationalist right wing of the Conservative Party. Indeed, political economic nationalism is also shared by the far right and the far left in various countries, if only because both share the view that the Common Market and other Western international ties and NATO not the least among them are an international obstacle to the revolution or counter-revolution that they seek to promote, and more easily so at home than in a larger political economic region.

This narrowing nationalist tendency on the right and left also extends to the United States ("America first" at both ends of the political spectrum) and to various regions and ethnic movements throughout Europe, such as in Basque Euzcadi, Bretagne, Waloonia, Kosivo, etc.

The domestic political economic response to the economic crisis in the West has been to abandon Keynesian demand management and to bid welfare farewell (Frank 1980 and 1982) and in the East to question Soviet style economic planning and introduce increasing privatisation of the economy. On both sides of the Elbe, and of course elsewhere as well, the economic crisis has placed all kinds of economic austerity measures on the order of the day. More often than not the implementation of economic austerity has required an increased measure of political repression, which in Europe has reached its most dramatic forms in Poland and Turkey. In Western Europe, now excepting (temporarily?) France, and of course in the United States, these political economic adjustments to the economic crisis have been accompanied by a marked shift of the political and ideological centre of gravity to the right (Frank 1980 Chapter 3). This political shift exacerbates the economic polarisation already engendered by the crisis and further shifts the economic burden of the crisis on the poor who can least afford to bear it. Though this domestic class struggle has led to some outbursts of labour militancy and ethnic/race rebellion, the former is undermined by the weakened bargaining power of labour through unemployment and the latter (as well as in part the former) are countered through increased legal and police repression. Often the militant and political protest movements are deflected, or sought to be deflected from and by their class targets, through appeals to nationalism. This was most vividly the case in the war over the Falklands/Malvinas Islands, but nationalist appeals also take many less belligerent forms of beclouding the class struggle.

In the face of heightening economic competition for markets, mounting or recurrent balance of trade and payments deficits, and growing unemployment in the West and some of the same and other problems in the East, existing governments in Europe and America of course are also falling prey to increasing pressures to rely on protectionist and other nationalist measures. In Eastern Europe, various countries have imposed export restrictions on each others citizens and tourists, while CMEA (Comecon) industrial divisions of labour are increasingly difficult to agree upon and implement. In Western Europe, the EEC Common Market and especially its Common Agricultural Policy (CAP) is subjected to recurrent and increasing strains as Britain and Germany object to the contributions they are obliged to make to sustain agricultural subsidies, especially in France, which wages wine wars with Italy and mutton or apple battles with Britain. The EEC steel war with the United States is in part the internationalisation of the intra-EEC battles over steel export and import quotas within the Common Market. National labelling, packaging, "safety" and other regulations are increasingly used to protect not so much the domestic consumer as the national producer against EEC and EFTA partners (ERA 1981). The European Monetary System (EMS) has not expanded to include the British pound and other currencies and is itself under the threat of breakdown through the chronic weakness of the French and Belgian francs. The expansion of the Common Market to incorporate more of Southern Europe is stalled and has become the source of additional strain within the EEC itself, while the European Parliament fulfils largely decorative functions. The exacerbation of these political economic nationalist pressures and tendencies in response to deepening world economic and domestic political crisis is a real possibility and could lead to the *de facto* or even *de jure* breakdown of the EEC and/or the CMEA and heightened international conflict in Europe.

Indeed, a world wide financial crash and breakdown of the international trade system are real possibilities, both separately and even more so together. Despite their far-reaching implications for the problematique and policy alternatives considered in this essay, a detailed analysis of this threat is beyond our scope here. Therefore, we confine ourselves to the review of a few newspaper headlines that reveal some of the circumstances and opinions at issue.

The first GATT ministerial level conference in a decade took place in Geneva in November 1982 amid sharpening disputes about trade policy among the giants of the world economy, the United States, the European Economic Commission, and Japan about "safeguard" protectionist measures against each other, American attempts to destroy the sacrosanct West European Common Agricultural Policy, and American led North-South disputes about whether or not to bring the increasingly lucrative banking and other service sectors under GATT rules. The press speculated: "Heading for a Trade War? A GATT meeting this week may be the last chance to slow the worst protectionist wave since the 1930s" (*Newsweek*, 29 November, 1982); "A last stand against the forces of protectionism" (*The Guardian*, 16 November, 1982); "GATT's finger in the dam against rising world protectionism" (*Financial Times*, 15 November, 1982). The mid-conference verdicts, as it was repeatedly prolonged to avoid a deadlock, and the post mortems were: "GATT conference faces collapse" (*Financial Times*, 27 November, 1982), "Participants Are Skeptical of Effect on Protectionism" (*International Herald Tribune*, 30 November, 1982). The next day, the *International Herald Tribune* (1 December, 1982) ran an eight column banner headline announcing "GATT Meeting on Liberalising Trade May Have Helped Launch a Trade War". *The Guardian* (30 November, 1982) pronounced a "Verdict: death by slow strangulation". Others opined that "it is difficult to overstate the degree to which . . . [it] was a bust . . . perhaps the chief victims at Geneva . . . are the developing nations" (*International Herald Tribune*, 4-5 December, 1982). The relative losers were the United States and the "winners" who sacrificed the least, were the Europeans. Therefore, "Protectionist pressures [are likely to increase in US Congress as a result of the GATT ministerial conference" (*Financial Times*, 2 December, 1982).

A related problem, which threatens to accelerate or exacerbate the breakdown of the post-war international trade system, is the growing financial crunch, especially on the major Third World and East European debtor economies, and the increasing possibility of a financial crash with world wide repercussions. Next to such a crash the 1929 Wall Street crash and the 1931 collapse of the Kreditanstalt in Vienna could appear as a storm in a teacup. The reasons for the growing financial crunch and the immediate causes of a possible crash might be any one or a combination of many. The ones that have received most recent attention are related to Third World debt, particularly since first Argentina during the Malvinas/Falklands war, then Mexico since August 1982 and finally Brazil in late 1982 became unable to service their foreign debts as scheduled. The press headlines observe: "Fear of Widening World Debt Load Slows Down 2 Decades of Tumultous Growth" (*International Herald Tribune*, 29 November, 1982 special report on Euromarkets); "Trouble for world banking. Frail economies of Poland, Mexico provoke fear of chain-reaction failures" (*Minneapolis Star and Tribune*, 8 September, 1982); "Bank Lending Cuts: Third World growth rates threatened" (*Financial Times*, 11 October, 1982); "Former IMF Chief gives warning amid flurry of reassurances by bankers: Bank crisis could lead to real slump" (*Guardian*, 6 October, 1982); "International Banking: The Illusions are stripped away", "Holes in the supervisory net"; "Bankers meet in private summit on liquidity crisis" (*Financial Times*, 15, 17 and 27 October, 1982); "International debt crisis 'will hit industrial growth', US banker warns" (*Guardian*, 9 October, 1982). In short, the scenario is that the new debt crisis is reducing the banks' willingness to continue lending to Peter to enable him to pay Paul and for Mexico and Brazil to import industrial goods from each other and for both of them to pay for exports from the United States and Western

Europe, whose own growth rates are thereby put in check. The inability of one of these countries to pay, especially through the New York interbank clearing house CHIPS, and the inability or delay in launching a rescue operation internationally could launch a domino effect chain reaction of bank liquidity crises, defaults or failures around the world that could bring the whole world financial system crashing down like a house of cards — with incalculable effects on world trade and production, except that they too would break down and the first efforts to contain or to remedy the impact throughout the world would likely be further protectionist measures and attempts at economic bloc formation.

In the face of aggravation of the world economic crisis and the apparent bankruptcy of post-war Keynesian demand management remedies in the West, a succession and mix(up) of alternative political economic policies have been tried and/or proposed in the West, which may be roughly classified as follows: (1) national and/or regional and enterprise monpolistic competitive policies, often at beggar-my-neighbour expense, which have generated or aggravated the West-West conflicts of interest and policy disagreements reviewed above; (2) national monetarist policies of (largely unsuccessful) restrictive management of the national (but not international) money supply and government expenditure in virtually all Western countries, which have failed to achieve their stated objectives anywhere and have encouraged the de-industrialisation of the United States under Presidents Carter and Reagan and nearly achieved it in Britain under Prime Ministers Callaghan and Thatcher; (3) anti-state interventionist supply-side policies of tax reductions to stimulate private investment and productivity, which under their Reagonomic guise in the United States have contributed to monstrous budget deficits and significant upward re-distribution of income, but to no visible stimulation of business investment or effort; (4) interventionist supply-side macroindustrial state investment controls, proposed for the "re-industrialisation of America" by some

Democratic Party "neoliberals", like Senator Gary Hart and economist Lester Thurow, *Business Week*, and Felix Rohatyn's proposal to revive the Reconstruction Finance Corporation (RFC) of the 1930s as an "investor of last resort", and attempted in France by President Mitterrand's government intervention and nationalisation to upgrade the technological level of French industry, and in the special circumstances of Canada by Pierre Trudeau's constitutional reform efforts to capture Alberta's and some American oil companies' fortunes and funnel them through the federal government to Ontario and other industries and in general encouraged perhaps by the attractiveness of the "Japan, Inc." model; (5) neo-Keynesian government pump-priming proposals for social wage spending and employment creation on the national level, combined with support for national industry, as proposed by the Schmidt government in Germany in early 1982, or also combined with import controls as in the British Labour Left's alternative economic strategy (AES) supported by Tony Benn, and sometimes supplemented by macroindustrial investment controls as in the AES proposals and Mitterrand France, and/or increased arms expenditures as virtually everywhere; and (6) global Keynesianism, à la Brandt Report and other proposals to create and/or transfer Marshall Plan type purchasing power to the Third World so that it might be spent in and revive the industrial development in the West. The prospects for these policy options individually or in combination are not brilliant. The past and foreseeable consequences of the first three approaches to crisis management (beggar-my-neighbour, monetarist and anti-interventionist supply side policies) are visible throughout the West, including Giscard France and Schmidt Germany, Frazer Australia and Muldoon New Zealand, and elsewhere, but of course most vividly in and through the economies of the prime exponents of Reaganomics and Thatcherism. (Frank, 1982.)

The fourth and fifth policy options are presently being put to the acid test by France under the presidency of

Mitterrand. In particular, the short-term policy and prospects of the fifth policy, neo-Keynesianism are anything but encouraging. An early *Financial Times Survey* (25 November, 1981) observed: "President Mitterrand was elected to carry out the almost impossible task of restoring France to full employment in the midst of world recession. Six months into his term of office his administration is not unexpectedly floundering in its bid to achieve higher rates of growth without exacerbating inflation". Soon thereafter, with its seat in Paris the "OECD warns France ... with carefully worded scepticism about the likely results of France's current economic strategy ... One of the main reservations ... is that the international economic environment is unlikely to help ... A policy leading to an expansion of domestic demand would merely exacerbate an already serious balance of trade and payment situation ... Other hurdles which have to be overcome include a possible acceleration in inflation and a persistence of private industry's reluctance to invest". (*Financial Times*, 2 February, 1982.) Another half year later "France is now having to face up to the painful consequences of having pursued last year an expansionary economic policy at a time when her major trading partners were deflating. The unexpected [sic] extent to which France is out of step ... has badly thrown out the Government's economic calculation ... The scale on which there has been a haemorrhaging of France's foreign exchange reserves has greatly limited his room for manoeuvre". (*Financial Times*, 9 June, 1982.) The "increase in imports sucked in by the continued bouyancy of French consumer demand" forced the government into two major devaluations of the French franc; and the inflation in excess of its EEC partners (which reduces the competitiveness of French exports and which is also fed by higher import prices after devaluation) led to the imposition of a four month government freeze on wages and prices and the renewed cutback on social expenditures, the employers' contribution to which reduced their firms' competitiveness and investment. The

Financial Times (21 June, 1982) commented again on "France after Devaluation: Socialism with an austere face":

> "For the Socialist hierarchy (not to mention the Communists) it has been a bitter pill to find that the hopes of 12 months ago of charting an 'alternative' economic strategy towards higher growth and full employment have been so humiliatingly swallowed up by a second devaluation, expenditure cuts and prices and wages freeze".

But the only other alternative to these painful internal economic measures would have been the external one of withdrawing from the European Monetary System (EMS), which was recommended by some cabinet ministers but was rejected – so far – by President Mitterrand, who fears the Common Market and other international repercussions of such a step, but warned that he did not have a "religious attachment" to the EMS. Nonetheless, the following observations about Mitterrandomics Mark II 1982 vintage appear realistic: "Keynesianism in a new guise: 'We put our money not into demand, but into the supply side' . . . [moving] away from grants and subsidies towards tax incentives . . . which could have come out of a Conservative Party manifesto" (*Financial Times* 28 September, 1982). A "French union chief who believes wages must fall . . . says 'The loss of salary is the only possible serious position if you want to keep industry competitive' even in nationalised industry, which still practices the same capitalist style management as before" (*Financial Times* 2 December, 1982). "Now the socialists are taking on a different task. The consumer is being held down with a new austerity programme and industry is being force-fed funds to invest. The strategy, with its focus on nationalisation and planning, sounds new, enlightened and socialist – and, for Mr Mitterrand it is. But in a fundamental way, the policy is old, very French and liable to prove dangerously protectionist" (*International Herald Tribune* 1 December, 1982). The ruling that each imported Japanese video recorder must be individually inspected to clear customs in the small inland town of Poitiers is a vivid illustration of this protectionist stance.

This French experience with short term neo-Keynesian demand stimulation against the international economic and EEC tide need not have been unexpected in France or elsewhere. It does, however, vividly illustrate the severe limitations of Keynesianism today, and especially of *national* attempts to implement it alone. If this fact of life so severely limits the room for manoeuvre of relatively strong and prosperous France, what greater ills would it bode for a smaller country or economically still more foreign trade dependent and industrially much weaker Britain, even if the Labour Party took it out of the Common Market or the Labour Left (an unlikely event indeed) were to attempt the implementation of its AES? Didn't Chancellor Schmidt warn that Germany alone (or even with Japan) is not a strong enough locomotive to pull the world economy out of doldrums? Would a far weaker national economy be strong enough to pull even itself out of the doldrums — or in the case of Britain out of an industrial depression that exceeds even that of 1932?

To answer this question it is necessary to examine the prospects of the other longer leg of French economic policy, which is also a pillar of the British AES and is gaining more adherents in the United States the more Reaganomics fails to deliver the goods: a "macroindustrial" policy of state support for ailing industries and regions, for technological innovation, for domestic capital flows with foreign protection at home and competition abroad, and with suitable collaboration from business and labour, etc., as proposed in a study of *US Industrial Competitiveness*, published in July 1981 by the Office of Technology Assessment of the US Congress and perhaps mediated by a sort of RFC. The official in charge of this industrial policy in the Elysée Palace in Paris remarked on the "shift from an economy led by demand to one in which costs and quality have become all-important. To this extent the French Socialists are supply-siders . . . investment is the central element in this process" under Socialist guidance (*Financial Times*, 8 January, 1982). It is, of course, still too early to know what the outcome of this dirigiste supply-side policy will be in France which, after Japan, has initiated it, or perhaps later in America or Britain and Germany. The new link of the French research and industries ministries has been dubbed an incipient French version of the Japanese MITI superministry. However, even the relative success of Japan so far and the relative size of the American domestic economy leave ample room for caution about the extent to which it will be possible to go very far with macroindustrial policy on a strictly *national* political economic basis in an international economy. This limitation on national policy would obtain even more so in Europe and especially in its smaller countries and weaker economies. Indeed, the apparently increasingly stringent limitations on socialist economic and technological development in the Soviet Union and Eastern Europe, in each of their economies individually as well as through Comecon jointly suggest the rationality of examining this alternative for its flaws and considering other political economic alternatives as well.

A sixth alternative political economic strategy has, of course, been proposed by the Brandt Commission and others: a sort of global Keynesianism through a North-South – and in that case, why not, West-East – Marshall Plan on a global scale. Apart from the implausibility of getting political economic support for global Keynesianism worldwide at a time when national Keynesianism is being abandoned in one country after another and protectionism is spreading like wildfire, there are other serious problems with this proposal. (Frank 1981b.) The United States was able to administer the Marshall Plan in Western Europe after the war when American hegemony was unparalleled and unchallenged. But who would or could administer a global Marshall Plan today, when American hegemony is increasingly eroded and challenged? Indeed, the very malfunctioning of the Atlantic Alliance and the challenge of Japan, not to mention the East-West tensions, are an essential part of the crisis and of the inability so far to prevent it from deepening. How, then could this disharmony or market-anarchy — as Arrighi (in Amin, *et al* 1982) calls it — be transformed from being the problem or at least its manifestation to becoming the reason for its own solution? Through a strengthened and expanded International Monetary Fund — World Bank Group with Security Council police powers? That seems hardly realistic for the foreseeable future. Too many powerful political economic forces would be unwilling to play along in this ball game according to still non-existent rules (the United States even torpedoed the modest Law of the Sea Authority), and there would be no arbiter to blow the whistle on anyone who broke the rules or even refused to play at all and oblige them to comply. Potential recourse to force and war is too widespread.

Beyond the recourse to major war and/or the total breakdown of the international economic system, are there no other alternatives that might be both plausible in their appeal and practical in their interest and possible implementability? Is there no political economic strategy that avoids the Scylla of the present impracticality of a really alternative economic political and military international order and the Charybdis of ultimately impracticable national(ist) political economic policies which moreover enhance the danger of nuclear war? There may be some that could perhaps emerge out of the conflicts of interest and disagreements over economic and strategic policy reviewed above.

One such proposal is the creation of a "Fortress (Western) Europe" behind external tariff barriers. This seems to be the strategy recommended by the European Research Associates (ERA 1981) in their study of growing protectionism in the EEC and elsewhere, which threatens to break up the Common Market. But if growing protectionism is inevitable in the present economic climate, as they argue, then they suggest that it would be far more preferable to direct it outward from the EEC and EFTA, that is from all of Western Europe, to the rest of the world and maintain free trade within the region. In that case, the ERA proposal could also be extended to attempt the application of Mitterrand and Benn type economic nationalism (theoretically supported by the Cambridge Economic Policy Group's import and investment control proposals for the UK) not on the national levels that almost certainly condemn them to failure, but on a West European wide level.

The press reports some straws in the wind that indicate further thinking and possible moves in this direction. The *Financial Times* (30 November, 1982) carried an article by David Lea, the assistant general secretary of the British Trade Union Congress and joint secretary of its liaison committee with the Labour Party, entitled "Economic planning — there is no alternative", which stresses that planning has become economically and socially necessary because of the world economic crisis and "cannot and should not be confined to national economic blocs". Stuart Holland, British Labour MP and author of *Beyond Capitalist Planning* sets out a "New Strategy for Europe" in the *New Socialist* (November/December 1982) based on "planning by agreement: the European convergence" and joint "better-my-neighbour" reflation through which participating economies "could certainly go much farther before running into major financial constraints". Holland reports on a joint European economic project under elaboration by members of the executives of the socialist parties of Portugal, Spain, Italy, Greece, France, Belgium, the Netherlands, Sweden and Britain's Labour Party.*

Interest is not confined, however, to individuals from parties of the left but extends to governments of the right and the EEC Commission itself. John Palmer, the European editor of the *Guardian* (3 December 1982) reports that "the European Community is well down the road towards economic 'Fortress Europe' and may soon follow by asserting its autonomy in political and even security policy. The strains within this week's meeting of NATO defence ministers could not be hidden from view. And the Copenhagen summit discusses a German/Italian

*Published by Spokesman, March 1983 under the title, *Out of Crisis*, A Project for European Recovery.

plan encouraging ultimate European union which, stripped of its pious symbolism, will result in the EEC governments including security and disarmament within the ambit of Common Market political co-operation". Commenting on the same EEC Copenhagen summit, the *Financial Times* (6 December, 1982) observed "external pressures coupled with a persistently gloomy economic outlook are moulding a new unity on commercial issues among the Ten . . . There is growing support in Europe for the combination of protectionism at the EEC level and unrestricted free trade within the Community. This is thought to be the only practical way of coping with competition from Japan and the newly industrialised countries".

The same sentiment is reflected among some European government leaders and officials.

> "President Francois Mitterrand's Government, in a bid to arrange strategic marriages with eligible foreign consorts for state-owned enterprises in high-technology sectors is playing the European card for all it is worth . . . French officials believe that the extended world recession has made the EEC more amenable to the idea of European co-operation to fend off US and Japanese competition. The plan adopted at the EEC summit in Copenhagen to boost European industry is seen in Paris as proof of this. The programme includes the formula, officials admit, of greater trade liberalism within the Community, but a more protectionist policy externally. When President Mitterrand put forward similar ideas in the autumn of 1981, they recall, he was cold-shouldered" (*Financial Times*, 15 December, 1982).

> "EEC governments reached a remarkable degree of agreement in Brussels yesterday that the only viable means of halting, and eventually reducing, unemployment lies in a sustained attack on public deficits, inflation and excessive production costs . . . Yesterday's consensus on macro-economic policy was a remarkable change of opinion for Sir Geoffrey [Howe, British Chancellor of the Exchequer] who was alone in arguing the case against co-ordinated reflation at a similar meeting 18 months ago. But the move to austerity in France, changes of political complexion in the governments of Belgium, the Netherlands and Denmark, together with deepening economic crisis elsewhere, has swung the balance of economic orthodoxy within the EEC closer to the British position" (*Financial Times*, 17 November, 1982).

> "Chancellor Helmut Kohl recently stood on the steps of the

> European Parliament building here and declared his belief in 'a united states of Europe'. This went further than the ritual declarations of belief in building the community . . . His predecessor, Helmut Schmidt, was never so expansive" (*Financial Times*, 12 October, 1982).

The EEC Commissioner for Industry, Viscount Etienne Davignon argues for a movement "Towards a more united Europe", which must "wage battles on the world market" over the next 20 years in the new fields of information technology and biotechnology, but which nonetheless should not pin its hopes on export-led revival but on opening up Europe's internal market through the following keys: discouraging national protectionist measures; European specifications and standards to ensure preference to European goods; company law, taxation systems and community action to encourage the creation of European industrial companies; taking account of the European market as a whole and not just national markets; a European pool of telecommunications systems to replace existing state monopolies; and a European wide research and development strategy. "Without a European response the Commission believes that the Community is threatened with extinction. The important thing is to ensure that public money is injected into the national economies in accord with a coherent European strategy" Davignon writes (*Financial Times*, 13 December, 1982).

For the moment, not only at the EEC Commission but also in government cabinets and the board rooms of industrial companies that include privately and state owned firms, the emphasis is on European co-operation in the micro-electronic and information advanced technology fields.

> "Arriving at a common industrial policy that would relaunch the EEC's stagnating micro-electronics sector is an agreed priority of all member governments, but it is proving fraught with political difficulty. Yet the EEC governments are well aware that to leave the field open to the present market leaders of Japan and the US will ultimately cost more in economic slowdown and lost employment than would the depredations of the new 'smart' machinery on factory floor jobs" (*Financial Times*, 13 December, 1982).

Accordingly, a dozen of Europe's leading electronic groups have felt compelled to join together in a still pilot venture called ESPRIT, which stands for European Strategic Programme of Research in Information Technology, which is angling for some $2 billion from the EEC Commission support or about 2 per cent of the Community's budget. The companies include GEC, ICL and Plessey from Britain; Siemens, AES and Nixdorf from West Germany; Thompson-CSF, Honeywell-Bull and CIT-Alcatel from France. Olivetti and STET from Italy, and Philips from the Netherlands (*Financial Times*, 1 August, 1982). Though, as one of the participants warns, "there are plenty of hurdles before Esprit becomes a reality", some of the firms involved are also trying to proceed with research and production sharing that involve fewer of them.

Of course, in the absence of a single European state (whose creation is not yet on the horizon at a time of resurging nationalism), the achievement of such West European-wide economic co-operation would pose considerable difficulties, even if there are mutual interests in hanging together in order to avoid hanging separately. In addition to the intra-West European problems the construction of this Fortress (Western) Europe would generate or exacerbate external economic and political conflict: Western Europe would be increasingly cut off from its Third World and particularly Middle Eastern sources of supply and markets both by its own action and by the resultant enhanced competition from the US and Japan, who might be led to undertake a new political economic offensive in the Third World. Such a likelihood lends all the more weight to the argument for extending any possible such West European economic integration to embrace enhanced economic and political rapprochement with Eastern Europe and to some extent the Soviet Union, which from both the supply and demand side would offer the opportunity to construct an economically much more viable — and politically more stable? — All-European Fortress or Pan-European Entente.

The very increasing West-West dissension within the

Atlantic Alliance and NATO and the no doubt different but complementary economic and political difficulties emerging in Comecon and the Warsaw Pact countries combined with the potentially common European interest in a stable solution to the Middle East crisis – ensuring the steady flow of oil to all of Europe – not to mention the desire for peace and arms limitations in Europe, could perhaps provide the political economic basis for a major international and national political realignment and an alternative regional or economic bloc strategy, which might offer a realistic path between the impractical whole world harmonious political economic order and the impracticable disharmony of and dangers of national political economic competition. A Pan-European economic strategy or even bloc with ties to the Middle East and perhaps Africa could possibly provide the basis of sufficient mutual economic interest in enough economic and political class and national segments in both Western and Eastern Europe to reduce the tension between the two areas and be coupled with the de-nuclearisation of the region through the revival or modernisation of the Rapacki Plan that called for the latter a generation ago.

The political economic rapprochement of Western and Eastern Europe that proved to be beyond reach then may be more possible to grasp now that there are many real common (that is same) or at least mutual (that is parallel) economic and some political interests among powerful political economic class and national segments on both sides of the Elbe and particularly in Germany itself. Moreover, the growing conflicts within both the Atlantic Alliance and the Eastern Bloc and the underlying economic and political weakening of both of the American and Soviet "superpowers" relative to their respective economic and political allies on either side of the Elbe could enable important political and economic forces in each of the present four major regional groupings, Western Europe, Eastern Europe, and their no longer so big respective brothers in the United States and the Soviet Union able to consider an alternative East-West European economic and political rapprochement. Such a solution might perhaps not be ideally the most desirable, but it could become the practically second best and certainly the lesser evil solution to either the prolongation of the increasingly economically and politically untenable present trends within the various economies, societies and states; or to the other alternative political economic policies that range from totally impossible to construct in practice towards practically certain to totally destruct altogether.

As long as far-reaching global Keynesian demand management and supply-side *dirigisme* remain quite impracticable, and limited national Keynesian demand management and supply-side policies turn out to be impractical in a world economy, there is perhaps some practical room and plausible reason for a major regionally based European wide macroindustrial effort at combining state intervention in investment finance and decision for sale of output on a regional preference market in an international economy and some co-ordination of credit creation and the distribution of effective demand on a similar regional basis.

By cutting the Gordian knots of their separate political economic limitations both CMEA and EEC might be able to overcome their separate limitations through a more perfect West and East European economic union and political alliance. Expanding the boundaries of systems that can no longer operate within the confines of their old boundaries offers no guarantee of salvation but is at least as practical as breaking the systems down into little pieces. And when there is a real basis in mutual economic interest for the amalgamation or at least rapprochement of the two systems, as there is between the EEC and the CMEA, and the alternative is the possible nuclear destruction of both, there is more than enough reason to make the political effort. Significantly, this political effort also opens the door for important economic and political interest groups and the peace movements within Western Europe to join in a common cause or at least to forge a tactical alliance with (rather than as heretofore a strategic one against) each other. Of course, mutual economic interests do not provide or guarantee political agreement. But the replacement of economic conflict by some economic agreement of interests certainly removes some obstacles to and facilitates political rapprochement between East and West and collaboration in the West between the peace movement and some business as well as state interests. Moreover, within Eastern Europe some interests in favour of economic and political liberalisation, not to mention any peace movements there, could perhaps collaborate in this direction without thereby threatening the vital security interests of the Soviet Union (that is through the extension elsewhere of the Hungarian reform model). A favourable straw in the wind may be that French President Mitterrand, who excepting Britain's Mrs Thatcher has been the vocally most anti-Soviet European leader and who comes from the country with the least developed peace movement, "is seen as feeling its way towards a new relationship with the Eastern bloc during the current visit to Hungary . . . [which he] deliberately picked . . . His aim is to demonstrate that coolness towards the Soviet Union does not exclude developing relations with other Communist states. The visit is inevitably seen as opening the door to the resumption of more normal relations with Moscow. The difficulties over the gas pipeline . . . are also on the agenda (*Financial Times*, 8 July 1982).

Most significant is the important priority that the Social Democratic Brandt and Schmidt governments in West Germany have given to their "Ost-politik" toward East Germany and the continuation of this emphasis by the Christian Democratic government under Helmut Kohl (and von Weizsäcker in West Berlin). Schmidt observed after leaving the government that both East Berlin and Bonn are aware of the parallels of interest in economic co-operation and peacekeeping, and the East German leader Erik Honecker suggested that for the West "trade between East and West is the best job-creation programme there is" (*Financial Times* 16 December and 25 October, 1982).

Each of the present allies of Eastern and Western Europe may have at the very least lesser evil reasons to acquiesce in such a political economic realignment, especially if their vital interests are safeguarded in the process. The Soviet Union, for whom prolongation of the present is very costly, could find the economic burden of its support of Eastern Europe and of its military expenditures very much lightened by a European rapprochement, which would also reduce some of the sources of a political tension within the USSR. The mere weakening or breakup of NATO should offer the Soviet Union a significant enticement to go along with such a European rapprochement and could compensate for what might be a sort of political Finlandization of Eastern Europe, which need not threaten vital Soviet interests by turning against her.

The United States would find the apparently inevitable loss of its hegemony in Europe increasingly confirmed, but would be freed to shift its economic and political attention increasingly to the Pacific including parts of Latin America and Asia in whose direction powerful forces are drawing or leading important American political economic interests anyway. Moreover, the Americans would be liberated from a major basis of their all-consuming obsession with Soviet power and its supposed threat. To the extent that this Soviet threat were to persist, it would also be turned more towards Asia and the Pacific, where it could be checked through a further development of the Washington-Tokyo-Peking axis and their possible political economic collaboration in the Asia Pacific region.

Important economic and political interests in the United States, especially in newer technologically more advanced industries and the expanding "sunbelt" states in the South and West of the country, have for some time been pushing for a Pacific Rim strategy to replace the old transatlantic European ties. At the same time, Jacques Attali, Mitterrand's principal economic adviser and the organiser of the Versailles summit, suggests that in the course of the present world economic crisis the centre of the world system will shift from the Atlantic to the Pacific. Other emerging sentiment in the United States is reflected by former Under-Secretary of State George Ball writing in the *Washington Post* who criticises "the doctrine-according-to-Reagan . . . that the Soviet Union is to blame for all major world ills" and who argues that "if many Europeans now regard United States' policy as erratic and unpredictable . . . [and] no longer trust American judgement and good sense . . . they are right" (*International Herald Tribune*, 20-31 January, 1982). On the other hand, in the United States W.W. Rostow, who was former National Security Adviser to President Kennedy and Johnson (and whose brother Eugene was handling arms control for President Reagan) writing in the *New York Times* reflects the apparent readiness of influential circles in the United States to contemplate a significant change in "Dealing with Russia after Poland's Coup: A Plan for Entente in Europe":

> "Four historical processes make the continued acceptance of the division of Europe unwise, not merely for the West but also for the Soviet Union. First, the coming to maturity and responsibility of the generation in Eastern Europe born after World War II, to whom the present arrangement makes little sense . . . Second, powerful decelerating economic forces at work in the Soviet Union and Eastern Europe . . . Remedy requires, among other things, wider and more harmonious economic relation with the West, including increased flows of capital and technology . . . Third, the economic forces at work in the West as well as in the East dictate efforts of the highest seriousness to reduce defence spending. Fourth, there is a new generation in the West. . . . Young people in Western Europe and the United States are asking perfectly fair and understandable questions: Why should Germany not be unified? Why should the European continent be littered with American and Soviet nuclear weapons? Why should American and Soviet forces be stationed in Europe more than 37 years after the end of World War II? . . . The questions must be answered. What is needed now . . . is to allow Europeans, in both East and West, to organise themselves more as Europeans; to ensure continued security for the So;viet Union and the United States, with reduced but not totally eliminated involvement in the military affairs of Europe . . . that would reduce the level of the European armed forces in both NATO and the Warsaw Pact countries; . . . strategically balanced US and Soviet

military force withdrawals from Europe; ... provisions for heightened multilateral economic co-operation within Europe. This would ensure, among other things, that a powerful united Germany would not seek to establish hegemony on the Continent. ... Others in the Soviet Union would seize on the prospect ... to achieve the abiding Soviet dream of a Western Europe cut off from the military support of the United States. They would be supported by a few Americans who have long hankered to cut West Europe loose. ... But without such an agreed vision and plan, Western policies are unlikely to be stable, patient and effective". (*New York Times/International Herald Tribune*, 26 January, 1982.)

In conclusion it appears that the natural course of world capitalist development and its renewed structural crisis are undermining the economic basis of and generating ever sharper political conflict within the Atlantic Alliance. Increasingly this dissent also covers strategic issues of relations with the Soviet Union and its allies in Eastern Europe. This area is also facing increasing economic and political problems in part because of the world economic crisis.

The combination of these Western and Eastern political economic problems poses serious dangers for the stability and peace of the world based on the bi-polar Mutual Assured Destruction (MAD) and nuclear parity faceoff between NATO and the Warsaw Pact. But the same political economic forces that pose this danger also offer the opportunity — the Chinese ideographs for crisis are a combination of those for danger and for opportunity — to forge a new multi-polar balance of power including a possible Pan European political economic entente to stabilise the strategic balance at least in the European theatre. Moreover, this possibility can become a more practical proposition insofar as the combination of the economic crisis in the West and in the East and their effects of undermining the economic basis of the Atlantic and Soviet-East European Alliances also provide a new economic basis for the tactical if not strategic co-operation of the peace movement and powerful political economic interests (and therefore the at least grudging acceptance or even support of the former by the latter) in Europe

West and East and even the acquiescence in the same by influential forces in the United States and the Soviet Union. The implementation of such global political economic realignments would not eliminate East European and Third World dependence any more than alternative realistic proposals would. Compared to the in any case untenable status quo and other alternative policies, however, the proposed world realignment centering on a Pan-European entente would offer greater hope for the achievement of important and widely shared desires: maintenance of world peace or at least avoidance of nuclear war, greater possibilities for economic growth in Western Europe, wider opportunities for national independence and political liberalisation in Eastern Europe, and increased political bargaining power and room for manoeuvre for socialist and nationalist liberation movements in the Third World South.

References cited

(other than newspapers, documents, etc., detailed in the text)

Amin, Samir (1982) and Giovanni Arrighi, André Gunder Frank and Immanuel Wallerstein, *Dynamics of Global Crisis*, New York, Monthly Review Press and London, Macmillan Press.

ERA-European Research Associates (1981) *EEC Protectionism: Present Trends and Future Practice*, 29 Boulevard Clovis, Brussels 1040.

Frank, André Gunder (1980) *Crisis: In the World Economy*, New York, Holmes & Meier and London, Heinemann.

__________ (1981a) *Crisis: In the Third World*, New York, Holmes & Meier and London, Heinemann.

__________ (1981b) *Reflections on the World Economic Crisis*, New York, Monthly Review Press, London, Hutchinson.

__________ (1981c) Contribution to Friedrich Ebert Foundation, ed. *Towards One World? International Responses to the Brandt Report*, London, Temple Smith.

__________ (1982) "After Reaganomics and Thatcherism, What? From Keynesian Demand Management via Supply-Side Economics to Corporate State Planning and 1984", *Contemporary Marxism* (San Francisco) No.4, winter.

Kaiser, Karl, Winston Lord, Therry de Montbrial, David Watt (1981) *Western Security: What has Changed? What should be done?* A Report prepared by the Directors of Forschungs Institut der Deutschen Gesellschaft für Auswärtige Politik (Bonn), Council on Foreign Relations (New York) Institut Francais des Relations Internationales (Paris), Royal Institute of International Affairs (London) with the assistance of an Advisory Group, New York and London, Council of Foreign Relations and Royal Institute of International Affairs, 1981.

Kendrick, John W. (1981) "International Comparisons of Recent Productivity Trends" in William Fellner, ed. *Essays in Contemporary Economic Problems, Demand, Productivity and Population*, Washington, DC, American Enterprise Institute.

Office of Technology Assessment (1981) US Industrial Competitiveness: A Comparison of Steel, Electronics, and Automobiles, Washington, Congress of the United States.

UNECE (1982) United Nations Economic Commission for Europe, Economic Survey of Europe in 1981, Prepublication Text of Chapter 3, Geneva, ECE (XXXVII/1 Add.1).